CHILDREN'S BOOKS TOO GOOD TO MISS

Children's Books Too Good To Miss

REVISED AND ENLARGED EDITION

MAY HILL ARBUTHNOT / MARGARET MARY CLARK
RUTH M. HADLOW / HARRIET G. LONG

1971
THE PRESS OF CASE WESTERN RESERVE UNIVERSITY
Cleveland & London

Sixth edition, revised, 1971.
Second printing.
First edition, 1948; second edition, 1953; third edition, 1959;
fourth edition, 1963; fifth edition, 1966.
Printed in the United States of America.
International Standard Book Number: 0-8295-0184-3.
Library of Congress Catalogue Card Number: 72-99225.

To the memory of
MAY HILL ARBUTHNOT

Prepared By

May Hill Arbuthnot, former associate professor of education, Flora Stone Mather College of Western Reserve University; author of *Children and Books, Time for Poetry, Time for Fairy Tales, Time for True Tales and Almost True, The Arbuthnot Anthology,* and *Children's Reading in the Home;* co-author with Shelton L. Root of *Time for Poetry,* 3d edition, and with Dorothy M. Broderick of *Time for Biography* and *Time for Stories of the Past and Present,* and of other forthcoming books published by Scott, Foresman and Co.

In 1959 the Women's National Book Association awarded to Mrs. Arbuthnot the Constance Lindsay Skinner Medal for distinguished contribution to the field of books. Western Reserve University bestowed upon her the honorary degree of Doctor of Humane Letters, 1961, and in 1964 she was awarded the Regina Medal of the Catholic Library Association. In 1969 the May Hill Arbuthnot Honor Lectureship was established, based on an annual grant by Scott, Foresman and Co. and to be administered by the Children's Services Division of the American Library Association. The lectures will be given in April of each year and followed by publication.

Mrs. Arbuthnot died October 2, 1969.

Margaret Mary Clark, head of the Lewis Carroll Room, Cleveland Public Library; lecturer in children's literature, Western Reserve University, 1949 to 1955; author of *Keeping Up With Children and Books,* published by Scott, Foresman and Co.; past chairman, Children's Services Division, American Library Association.

Ruth M. Hadlow, coordinator, Work With Children, Cleveland Public Library; past chairman of the Service to Children Round Table, Ohio Library Association; member of the Newbery-Caldecott Awards Committee, 1969-70, Children's Services Division, American Library Association.

Harriet G. Long, professor emeritus, School of Library Science, Western Reserve University; author of *Rich the Treasure: Public Library Service to Children,* published by the American Library Association, and *Public Library Service to Children: Foundation and Development,* published by the Scarecrow Press in 1970.

Foreword

If one man's meat is another man's poison, certainly one man's book may be another man's boredom. Nowhere are individual tastes more pronounced than in the field of reading. There is probably not a single book that a group of fifty adults would agree upon as a favorite, and the older the children the more nearly this is true of them also. The youngest might stand united in their devotion to *Mother Goose* and *Peter Rabbit*, but with older children there would be no such agreement. One child might put *Alice in Wonderland* at the top of his list of favorites while another would omit *Alice* entirely. Does this mean, if *Alice* is omitted from many lists, that we should no longer include *Alice* in our book offerings for children? Probably not, but it certainly does mean that we should scrutinize rather carefully the causes for its omission. Was it given to children when they were too young to be amused by its logical daftness, or when it was too difficult for them to read, or did they just miss exposure to *Alice* all along the way? Perhaps they would not have enjoyed *Alice* anyway; perhaps they were young realists with minds geared to science and machinery. But would they not have a chance of growing up to be better balanced human beings for having chuckled over Tweedledum and Tweedledee or the Mad Hatter's tea party?

This is a speculative question, of course, but there seem to be, in the great flood of children's books from the advent of *Alice in*

Wonderland, Tom Sawyer, and *Little Women,* certain timeless books whose appeal never diminishes. Some of these have become a part of our vocabularies, our codes of ethics, our standards of family life, our inner world of fancy, or fun, or sheer beauty. *Mother Goose, The Three Little Pigs, Millions of Cats, The Snow Queen, Heidi, The Jungle Books,* these and others constitute a literary heritage which we should not like children to miss, even though we realize that not every child will enjoy all of them. Nor should we expect them to. All we ask is that children be exposed to these choice books with the privilege of rejecting those they do not enjoy. Heaven forbid that any child should come to detest a good story or a delightful book of poetry because it was forced upon him. It will, however, be a rare child indeed who through the years does not develop some favorites among these fine books, provided he meets them at approximately the right time for him.

Lists of good books for children are almost as numerous as children, in spite of which there seem to be compelling reasons for this one. The first reason for this list is that the influx of new books for children is so staggering each year, and their pictorial appeal is so potent, that old favorites are being crowded out. The new books which replace them may or may not have equal significance. Age is no guarantee of excellence, nor are beautiful illustrations and recency any indication of triviality. There are plenty of old books for children which are much better forgotten and many new books of such unique and fresh distinction that they have about them all the earmarks of a classic except age. The question is, with new books inundating the bookshelves, who has time to remember that every generation of children revels in *The Tale of Peter Rabbit* and *The Adventures of Robin Hood*? Who is going to see that each new crop of children has a chance to encounter these old favorites at the right age? Who has time to scan critically the masses of new books and to watch, over a period of years, the children's responses to them in order to determine which of the hundreds seem likely to make the list of permanent favorites for a large number—never all—but a large number of children?

Teachers and children's librarians are in a strategic position to perform these services, and for this reason a group of us, whose work involves both children and children's books, became actively interested in the problem of determining which books every child should at least have a look at. We asked ourselves, first, which of the old books, the so-called children's classics, should each new generation of children be exposed to and at approximately what age? Second, which of the recent books show signs of possessing not only literary distinction but permanent child appeal? Rereading books for children over a period of several years, we weighed them for certain qualities.

First, we asked, *is the book good literature?*
That is, does the text stand up of itself, regardless of illustrations? Has it distinction of theme and style?

To answer this question we read aloud certain debatable books. Some of our favorites we discovered were pictorial lyrics but textual monotones. In short, the illustrations were carrying the story. On the other hand, we found many a text, *Ferdinand,* for instance, and *The Little House,* equally good without their charming pictures. This experiment of reading a story without showing the pictures was sometimes tried with the children. In Wanda Gag's *Millions of Cats,* for instance, the pictures are small and not easily seen in a large group of children, but it was found that the story captivates them just the same. We admit that this standard of literary quality is subjective, but we are trained workers in this field, and recognizing the fact that specialists in any field—literature or medicine—do disagree, we tried to be reasonable. We listened to opposed points of view, we evaluated them and then re-evaluated books after a lapse of time, and finally we accepted a majority vote after all opinion and all records had been considered.

Second, we asked, *does the book make a significant contribution to the child's wisdom, or merriment, or appreciation of beauty?*

Some books broaden a child's horizons, give him new sympathies and understanding, open his insight into human relationships. Most good stories provide him with clear standards of right and wrong, show him the conflicts and ethics of human behavior.

Other books provoke spontaneous and wholesome laughter. Still other books, especially books of poetry, have the power of opening the child's eyes to the wonder and beauty of the world.

To determine whether a book has the power to perform any or several of these services, we considered records of home, public library, and classroom discussions; children's spontaneous responses to a book; their requests to have it again or to talk about it; the questions it provoked; the children's subsequent references to it, or their indifference. We also considered the testimonial of adults concerning their own responses to certain books read or listened to in childhood and still enjoyed in retrospect. Such books we ourselves reread and tried again with children. The recent books in the list are not too recent. Most of them have been acclaimed by large numbers of children over a period of at least two or three years. They have also been praised by numerous experts in the field of children's literature. While this is not an inclusive list, it is, we think, a wholesome balance between the old and the new, as well as an interesting cross section of different types of children's literature: fiction, poetry, biography. We have made no attempt to evaluate informational books in any field.

Finally, we asked, *does the book have child appeal?*
This appeal may be obvious and instantaneous, upon first reading or hearing, or its hold on the children may develop slowly, only after several hearings.

This last point is so important and so continuously overlooked that we need to consider it in relation to the whole list.

Some stories and some verses make a quick appeal just as some popular music does. Such literature includes excellent materials and others which are trivial and banal. On the other hand, certain stories and poems must be heard repeatedly before the pattern or significance of the whole can be appreciated. The fact that complete enjoyment of a book is slow in arriving does not mean that it is not worth struggling for. Rather, we should remember the patient assistance the schools give children in the development of a taste for symphonic music. It takes time, but if even a few children are carried from a limited enjoyment of only the most obvious popular tunes to a life-long ability to enjoy great music, it is well worth all of the effort involved. The same process is needed with some literature. All poetry, beyond the lightest of light verse, and such examples of exquisite prose as Kenneth Grahame's *Wind in the Willows*, must be heard and heard again, lived with, mulled over, and savored slowly to be appreciated. Yet most children, who would not have the patience or the imagination to discover such literature for themselves, enjoy fine poetry when it is read to them unaffectedly and well, and a child or two in every group will probably love *Wind in the Willows* as long as he lives if it has been read aloud to him by someone who loves it too.

To judge, then, the child-appeal of books, we consulted various sources. We scanned library records of children's voluntary withdrawals of books. Those topping such records in several cities would seem to be favorites. Whether or not they were good literature was another matter. We looked at the listings of books in such bibliographies as those made by the *American Library Association, The Association for Childhood Education, National Council of Teachers of English,* and *School Library Journal, Junior Libraries, The Horn Book,* and the *Bulletin of the Center for Children's Books,* University of Chicago. We used teachers' records of children's favorite books throughout our large public school system, and we consulted gifted storytellers in schools and libraries concerning the children's responses to and requests for stories and poems.

Nevertheless, in spite of our conscientious efforts to use available data from as many different sources as possible, this list does not represent a statistical research for children's favorite reading. It represents the judgment of a group of specialists, working with children and children's books over a considerable period of years, trying to determine which of the old books should be salvaged because of their rich significance for children today and which, out of the multiplicity of new books, should be cherished for the same reasons. This means, of necessity, a somewhat subjective rating of these books.

This list is brief. You will miss some of your favorites, but even as it stands not every child is going to enjoy every one of these books. All we are trying to suggest is that here is an irreducible minimum of books which every child should be exposed to and helped to enjoy. If he rejects some of them, that is his privilege. At least we are giving him a chance to see and hear fine literature, to browse around, to select and reject on his own. Some of these books, discovered in childhood, will be cherished always. In some of them a child will find laughter, in others heroism, beauty, dreams. If some children never develop the capacity to enjoy fine books, the list will still be worthwhile if it helps other children to discover literature they might have missed, literature which opens their eyes to the joy of reading, to the power and glory of books.

A revision of this list is essential at this time, because some of the recommended books are now out of print and some new books have deserved inclusion. This revision includes almost three hundred titles and has permitted the addition of forty more titles and editions. Even so, the list is brief.

May Hill Arbuthnot

Children's Book Awards

THE CALDECOTT MEDAL

The Caldecott Medal is named in honor of Randolph Caldecott, an English artist who pioneered in book illustrations for young children between 1878 and 1885. It has been awarded annually since 1938 by Frederick G. Melcher, editor of *Publisher's Weekly,* for the most distinguished picture book for children. Since Mr. Melcher's death in 1963, his son, Daniel Melcher, has continued the award.

THE NEWBERY MEDAL

The Newbery Medal is named in honor of John Newbery, a London bookseller of the eighteenth century. It has been awarded annually since 1922 by Frederick G. Melcher to the author of the most distinguished contribution to children's literature, and since 1963 his son, Daniel Melcher, has continued the award.

A candidate for either of these awards must be a citizen or a resident of the United States, and the book must have its first publication in the United States. The awards are made annually by the Children's Services Division of the American Library Association.

Contents

CHILDREN'S BOOKS TOO GOOD TO MISS

For Children Under 6

PICTURE STORIES

1. LITTLE TIM AND THE BRAVE SEA CAPTAIN   Walck
Edward Ardizzone
Illustrated by the author

A large book about the large adventures of a small boy! How Tim goes
to sea, weathers a wreck, and comes home in triumph is told with a
casual air that is entirely convincing. Fine sea pictures add to the
unusual qualities of an excellent story.

2. MADELINE   Viking
Ludwig Bemelmans
Illustrated by the author

Life in a Paris school for little girls follows a pleasant pattern, and there
is calm and security within its vine-clad walls until one night small
Madeline interrupts the traditional routine. The story, told largely in
pictures, is colorful and highly amusing. For the slightly older child, a
Christmas holiday in the Austrian Tyrol is described with refreshing
zest in the author's HANSI.

3. MIKE MULLIGAN AND HIS STEAM SHOVEL   Houghton Mifflin
Virginia Lee Burton
Illustrated by the author

Mike and his unwanted, outmoded steam shovel, Mary Ann, dig a new
and unusual home for themselves in the town of Popperville. A picture
story which combines realistic and imaginative elements with humor
and appeal.

4. THE HAPPY LION
McGraw-Hill
Louise Fatio
Illustrated by Roger Duvoisin

So long as the Happy Lion sat peacefully in his little park, everyone in the French village loved him. But when, one day, he went for a stroll through the streets, no one said, "Bonjour Happy Lion"; in fact his best friends fled wildly in every direction, all except one. The happy ending to this gay tale is entirely plausible, and the witty, colorful illustrations by Roger Duvoisin add to the fun and make the French village as familiar as Main Street.

Marjorie Flack: 5-6

5. ASK MR. BEAR
Macmillan
Illustrated by the author

A little boy did not know what to give his mother for her birthday, but when he asked Mr. Bear, he received a surprising suggestion that was just right. Clear-colored pictures add to the charm of this favorite story of the two- and three-year-olds. Miss Flack's "Angus" books are equally beloved. No one has done better realistic picture stories for children two to seven than this skillful author-artist. ANGUS AND THE DUCKS, ANGUS AND THE CAT, and ANGUS LOST are published by Doubleday.

6. THE STORY ABOUT PING
Viking
Illustrated by Kurt Wiese

A naughty little duckling ventures away from his family and home on a Chinese houseboat. Colorful illustrations by Kurt Wiese and a humorous text make this a good animal story and a delightful introduction to Chinese life.

7. MILLIONS OF CATS
Coward-McCann
Wanda Gág
Illustrated by the author

The little old man unwisely chose not one, but "millions and billions and trillions" of cats to keep his lonely wife company at home, with somewhat startling results. A nonsense tale filled with gay repetitive rhymes and illustrated with black-and-white drawings.

8. THE SNOWY DAY   Viking
   Ezra Jack Keats
   Illustrated by the author

The solitary play of a three- or four-year-old boy on a snowy day reflects the experiences any small child might have; only the illustrations show that he is a Negro child. The uncluttered pictures, part watercolor, part collage, establish the mood and illustrate the story with rare beauty. *Caldecott Medal, 1963.* WHISTLE FOR WILLIE, in which a small boy learns to "pucker up" his lips and whistle for his dog, is another book by this gifted artist. In PETER'S CHAIR (Harper & Row), Peter reluctantly yields his beloved chair, now too small, to Susie, his baby sister.

9. MAKE WAY FOR DUCKLINGS   Viking
   Robert McCloskey
   Illustrated by the author

Aided by an Irish policeman, Mr. and Mrs. Mallard and their eight ducklings waddle sedately through the busy traffic of Boston's streets to the Public Gardens, where peanuts and popcorn are plentiful. Perhaps no other author-illustrator for young children has captured so well the flavor of America and the brand of humor that is peculiarly our own. *Caldecott Medal, 1942.* BLUEBERRIES FOR SAL is an equally popular picture tale.

10. THE TALE OF PETER RABBIT   Warne
    Beatrix Potter
    Illustrated by the author

Disobedient Peter loses his fine clothes and almost ends as a rabbit pie when he ventures into Farmer MacGregor's forbidden garden.Distinctive writing and a strong appeal to a small child's sympathies and sense of justice make this an outstanding story. The watercolor illustrations add charm to the narrative by their simplicity of detail and delicacy of color. First published in 1903. BENJAMIN BUNNY, JEMIMA PUDDLE-DUCK, and SQUIRREL NUTKIN are a few of the author's other titles.

11. WHERE THE WILD THINGS ARE   Harper & Row
Maurice Sendak
Illustrated by the author

His wolf costume inspires small Max to such boisterous play that he is ordered to bed. Suddenly the walls of his room disappear, and Max finds himself sailing off to a forest of strange wild creatures who acclaim him their king. Hunger makes Max abandon his royal role, and back he sails, awakening in his own bed and ready for supper. A lyrically told tale of a small rebel and his compensating dream. The illustrations are bizarre and imaginative. *Caldecott Medal, 1964.*

12. WHITE SNOW, BRIGHT SNOW   Lothrop, Lee & Shepard
Alvin Tresselt
Illustrated by Roger Duvoisin

The approach of the first snowfall of winter is forecast by the postman, the policeman, the farmer, and the rabbit—all friends of the young child. The description of winter activities and the changes brought about by the coming of spring are told in rhythmic prose that is not only beautiful and vivid but also childlike in its simplicity. *Caldecott Medal, 1948.* Clear-colored pictures add to the charm of this book, and also to SUN UP, RAIN DROP SPLASH, and HIDE AND SEEK FOG by the same author.

ALPHABET BOOKS

ABC books are exceedingly useful for young readers and often prove fascinating to the child in the prereading stage.

13. JOHN BURNINGHAM'S ABC   Bobbs-Merrill
John Burningham
Illustrated by the author

Bold, colorful illustrations, representing for the most part objects familiar to the younger child, make this a distinctive introductory alphabet book.

14. ABC BUNNY   Coward-McCann
Wanda Gág
Illustrated by the author

The rhyming text of this enchanting alphabet has a continuity unusual in ABC books, and there is humor in the unexpected conclusion. One scarlet capital on each page accents the large, dark, superb lithographs. He is a fortunate child who learns his alphabet from this book.

15. ALL AROUND THE TOWN   Lippincott
Phyllis McGinley
Illustrated by Helen Stone

The poems which accompany each letter are witty and sometimes lovely enough to use for themselves alone. Aided by the fine illustrations of Helen Stone, the verses cover the city sights and sounds which most interest children. Moreover, whether the little poems are about "the bouncing bus" or "the jumping jay walker," they present the letters of the alphabet with a masterly use of the phonetics of each letter.

16. BRUNO MUNARI'S ABC
Bruno Munari
Illustrated by the author

World

This artist designs books for children with little content but striking beauty. The large pages make effective use both of clear colors and white space. "F a Fly a Flower a Feather more Flies and a Fish" starts a fly on its way, and it zooms happily through the book to the last page. Such an ABC book has a sensory rather than an ideational appeal and is better, perhaps, for the youngest children but is superb eyetraining for every age.

17. BRIAN WILDSMITH'S ABC
Brian Wildsmith
Illustrated by the author

Watts

One of the most beautiful alphabet books for children, it uses pages in solid colors, rich harmonizing tones of purple, blue, orange, green, rose, and many more, each illustrated with an animal or familiar object and single-word text.

FOLK TALES AND FABLES

CHICKEN LITTLE (or HENNY PENNY)
GINGERBREAD BOY
LITTLE RED HEN AND THE GRAIN OF WHEAT
THE PANCAKE
Cumulative folk tales which delight small listeners because of the repetition of sound and action.

THE THREE BEARS
THE THREE BILLY GOATS GRUFF
THE THREE PIGS
Animal tales are early favorites. In the titles listed, repetition pleases the ear, and dramatic action brings a satisfying sense of wonder and surprise. Suggested sources:

18. TOLD UNDER THE GREEN UMBRELLA   Macmillan
    *Association for Childhood Literature, International Literature
    Committee, compiler.*
    Illustrated by G. Gilkison

Illustrated by L. Leslie Brooke: 19-20

19. STORY OF THE THREE BEARS   Warne

20. STORY OF THE THREE LITTLE PIGS   Warne

21. CHIMNEY CORNER STORIES   Putnam's
    Veronica Hutchinson, compiler
    Illustrated by Lois Lenski

22. THE LION AND THE RAT   Watts
    La Fontaine
    Retold and illustrated by Brian Wildsmith

23. THE COCK, THE MOUSE, AND   Macrae Smith
    THE LITTLE RED HEN
       Félicité Lefèvre
       Illustrated by Tony Sarg
The beloved repetitive tale of the wise little hen who saved her
companions from the wicked fox is doubly appealing in this large-print
edition which retains the colorful Tony Sarg illustrations. Originally
published in 1907.

RHYMES AND POETRY

24. SUNG UNDER THE SILVER UMBRELLA   Macmillan
Illustrated by Dorothy Lathrop

Association for Childhood Education, International Literature Committee, compiler.

An anthology of authentic poetry for children from four to eight years old, which contains a varied and distinguished selection. Each group begins with the simplest poems for the youngest and progresses to more difficult examples. The collection contains nonsense verse, fine lyric poetry, free verse, Japanese hokku, and several Psalms. Dorothy Lathrop's delicate pictures add to the charm of this unusual anthology.

25. FROG WENT A-COURTIN'   Harcourt Brace Jovanovich
John Langstaff, editor
Illustrated by Feodor Rojankovsky

Choice animal illustrations rich in colorful detail add to the charm of this version of the long popular ballad of Frog's wooing of little Miss Mousie. *Caldecott Medal, 1956.*

26. IN A SPRING GARDEN   Dial
Richard Lewis, editor
Illustrated by Ezra Jack Keats

> Just simply alive,
> Both of us, I
> And the poppy.
> —Issa

These brief lines exemplify the spirit of this fine introductory collection of twenty-eight haiku which follow a day in spring from a red morning sky to the passing of a giant firefly. The vivid collage and watercolor illustrations perfectly complement the verses. Older children and their parents will appreciate Mr. Lewis' THE MOMENT OF WONDER: A COLLECTION OF CHINESE AND JAPANESE POETRY.

Clement C. Moore: 27-28

27. THE NIGHT BEFORE CHRISTMAS Grosset & Dunlap
Illustrated by Leonard Weisgard

Christmas would be incomplete without this American classic. Santa, with his "sleigh full of toys and eight tiny reindeer," sailing through wintry skies, mounting to the housetops, popping down chimneys to fill waiting stockings—this Santa has become our national symbol of Christmas gaiety and giving. Children learn this long narrative poem with a few hearings and love it always. Originally published in 1823. Another attractive edition is:

28. THE NIGHT BEFORE CHRISTMAS Lippincott
Illustrated by Arthur Rackham

Mother Goose: 29-34

29. THE REAL MOTHER GOOSE Rand McNally
Illustrated by Blanche Fisher Wright

In 1965 the publishers issued a Fiftieth Anniversary Edition of this popular old book, with an introduction by Mrs. Arbuthnot concerning the history of the Mother Goose verses. Pictures are large, clear, and colorful, and there are over four hundred verses. It is a particularly useful edition with the youngest school children. Other editions are:

30. BOOK OF NURSERY AND Doubleday
MOTHER GOOSE RHYMES
Illustrated by Marguerite De Angeli

31. LAVENDER'S BLUE: A BOOK OF NURSERY RHYMES Watts
Kathleen Lines, compiler
Illustrated by Harold Jones

32. MOTHER GOOSE AND NURSERY RHYMES Atheneum
Illustrated by Philip Reed

33. THE MOTHER GOOSE TREASURY Coward-McCann
Illustrated by Raymond Briggs

34. RING O' ROSES   Warne
    Illustrated by L. Leslie Brooke

35. SING-SONG   Macmillan
    Christina Rossetti
    Illustrated by Marguerite Davis

Simple rhythmic verses about frisky lambs and merry children, the wind that "never rests," the caterpillar "brown and furry," and "timid, funny, brisk little bunny," who "winks his nose and sits all sunny." Unsurpassed in lyric quality and childlike spontaneity, these verses, originally published in 1872, are excellent to use following Mother Goose.

36. THE FOX WENT OUT ON A CHILLY NIGHT   Doubleday
    Illustrated by Peter Spier

The old folk song about the escapades of a hungry fox is introduced in handsome picture-book format, with illustrations rich in color and detail. Music is appended so that the short rhythmic verses can be sung or read.

Robert Louis Stevenson: 37-38

37. A CHILD'S GARDEN OF VERSES   Walck
    Illustrated by Tasha Tudor

Stevenson once said, "I am one of the few people in the world who do not forget their own lives." Because of the power he has of identifying himself with the child, his poems are beloved by English-speaking children everywhere. Originally published in England under the title PENNY WHISTLES in 1885. Another attractive edition is:

38. A CHILD'S GARDEN OF VERSES   Watts
    Illustrated by Brian Wildsmith

BIBLE STORIES

39. THE CHRIST CHILD Doubleday
Illustrated by Maud and Miska Petersham

In this picture book, which tells the story of the Nativity, it is indeed fortunate that the Petershams have used the biblical text with its poetic beauty and simple dignity. The illustrations interpret the spirit of the Holy Land with reverence, and their glowing colors delight the eye.

For Children 6, 7, and 8

PICTURE BOOKS AND STORIES

40. DASH AND DART   Viking
Conrad and Mary Buff
Illustrated by the authors

The first year in the life of twin fawns is simply and beautifully told. The forest magic of the illustrations, together with the cadenced prose of the text, make this a book to read aloud and to look at over and over again.

41. THE LITTLE HOUSE   Houghton Mifflin
Virginia Lee Burton
Illustrated by the author

The little house was very happy as she sat on the quiet hillside watching the changing seasons. As the years passed, however, tall buildings grew up around her, and the noise of city traffic disturbed her. She became sad and lonely until one day someone who understood her need for twinkling stars overhead and dancing apple blossoms moved her back to just the right little hill. The rhythmic quality of the text is beautifully reproduced in the illustrations by the author. *Caldecott Medal, 1943.*

42. DID YOU CARRY THE FLAG   Holt, Rinehart and Winston
    TODAY, CHARLEY?
    Rebecca Caudill
    Illustrated by Nancy Grossman

This is the question his parents, brothers, and sisters ask Charley each
day when the bus returns him from a summer school for four- and
five-year-olds. Unfortunately, Charley's curiosity always gets him into
trouble, and it is a long time before he wins the coveted honor. An
engagingly told story of a very real little boy who lives in the
Appalachian mountain country. Equally appealing is the author's A
POCKETFUL OF CRICKET, with the same regional background,
illustrated by Evaline Ness.

43. IN MY MOTHER'S HOUSE   Viking
    Ann Nolan Clark
    Illustrated by Velino Herrera

Written in poetic prose of disciplined simplicity, this book gives a
picture of our Plains Indians, their work, their communal life, and their
attitudes and ideals. Indian children helped the author to write the text,
and Velino Herrera, an Indian artist, drew the stylized pictures which
add to the charm and authenticity of the book.

44. HENRY HUGGINS   Morrow
    Beverly Cleary
    Illustrated by Louis Darling

A lively, humorous tale about Henry, a third-grader, and his dog, Ribsy,
who is his companion on many an escapade. The author's
understanding of small boys, their interests and activities, lends weight
to a book whose popularity, since it was first published in 1950, is
equalled by the several sequels which have followed it.

45. THE COURAGE OF SARAH NOBLE   Scribner's
Alice Dalgliesh
Illustrated by Leonard Weisgard

When her mother wrapped Sarah Noble in a warm new cloak, she said, "Keep up your courage, Sarah Noble." And eight-year-old Sarah had need of this advice, for she was journeying on foot into the wilderness with her father to cook and care for him. When unfriendly settlers scowled at her, or wolves howled near them in the forest, or Indians came near, Sarah hugged her cloak around her, remembered her mother's words, and managed to survive. Based on a true episode, this story of a child's fortitude is movingly told.

46. SNOW PARTY   Pantheon
Beatrice Schenk De Regniers
Illustrated by Reiner Zimnik

Snow-blocked roads lead hordes of unexpected visitors to the lonely little old man and woman on their prairie farm. The lively humor and rhythmic repetitiveness of this modern tale make it perfect to read aloud. Reiner Zimnik's black-and-white illustrations, which become increasingly crowded with every new arrival at the impromptu party, offer their own special entertainment for the observing child.

47. THE 500 HATS OF BARTHOLOMEW CUBBINS   Vanguard
Theodor Seuss Geisel (pseud. Dr. Seuss)
Illustrated by the author

One of the funniest tales of the last three decades! Bartholomew's hat troubles never lose their charm. As gravely told as a folk tale, the story's humor grows with each reading. There is grim suspense and a conclusion that satisfies everyone, including Bartholomew. Its sequel, BARTHOLOMEW AND THE OOBLECK (Random), is equally popular. Favorites with children under six are AND TO THINK THAT I SAW IT ON MULBERRY STREET (Vanguard) and the rhyming nonsense of HORTON HATCHES THE EGG (Random).

48. NEW ILLUSTRATED JUST-SO STORIES   Doubleday
    Rudyard Kipling
    Illustrated by Nicolas

Older children can read Kipling's JUST-SO STORIES for themselves, but this edition is particularly satisfying to young children because of its colorful picture-book format. When they hear the stories read aloud, they chuckle over the funny words and the sonorous sentences. JUST-SO STORIES was originally published in 1902.

49. THE STORY OF FERDINAND   Viking
    Munro Leaf
    Illustrated by Robert Lawson

What happens when a gentle bull who loves to smell flowers is goaded into temporary fierceness by the sting of a bee! Ferdinand's incongruous affection for flowers captured the public fancy three decades ago, and the children have loyally retained him as a favorite picture-book character.

50. WINNIE-THE-POOH   Dutton
    Alan A. Milne
    Illustrated by Ernest Shepard

Six-year-old Christopher Robin listens to stories about his toy pets, Rabbit, Piglet, Eeyore the Donkey, Kanga and Baby Roo, and especially about Winnie-the-Pooh, the Bear of Little Brain, one of the most captivating characters in children's literature. The magic of Mr. Milne's prose endows these playthings with distinct individuality, aided by Ernest Shepard's drawings, which are an integral part of the book. This is a prime favorite for reading aloud to the entire family. Followed by HOUSE AT POOH CORNER. THE WORLD OF POOH offers both these titles in a single, color-illustrated volume.

51. LITTLE BEAR   Harper & Row
    Else Minarik
    Illustrated by Maurice Sendak

This book and its successors—FATHER BEAR COMES HOME, LITTLE BEAR'S FRIEND, LITTLE BEAR'S VISIT—are among the chief charmers in the flood of easy-to-read publications. Little Bear and his mother are prototypes of any little boy and his loving mama. The stories center on Little Bear's play, but always the theme of Mother's understanding and love comes through with enough humor to prevent over-sweetness. Maurice Sendak's illustrations make the antics and charm of Little Bear irresistible.

52. MANY MOONS   Harcourt Brace Jovanovich
    James Thurber
    Illustrated by Louis Slobodkin

The little Princess Lenore, ill from a surfeit of raspberry tarts, lies in her huge, canopied bed and longs for the moon. Her worried father, the king, calls upon the members of his court to get it for her, but it is the court jester alone who understands the world of a child's imagination and saves the situation. This first book which James Thurber wrote for children is skillfully told with a special quality of tenderness and wisdom. The illustrations by Louis Slobodkin have the same elusive, individual quality as the text, and this happy union of author and artist creates a harmonious whole. *Caldecott Medal, 1944.*

53. THE BIGGEST BEAR   Houghton Mifflin
    Lynd Ward
    Illustrated by the author

Johnny Orchard never did acquire the bearskin for which he boldly went hunting. Instead, he brought home a cuddly bear cub, which grew in size and appetite to mammoth proportions and worried his family and neighbors half to death! An ingenuous and happy solution ends this highly humorous tale, which is superbly illustrated and ageless in appeal. *Caldecott Medal, 1953.*

54. CROW BOY   Viking
    Taro Yashima
    Illustrated by the author

Chibi, shy, lonely and afraid, walks daily to the village school from his Japanese farm home. An understanding teacher discovers his remarkable skill in imitating the sounds of the crows and helps make the class aware of it, too. On graduation day, Chibi is honored for his perfect attendance, and, best of all, his schoolmates greet him with the nickname Crow Boy in honor of his special talent. This appealing story, which reflects the experiences of many lonely children, is illustrated with colorful crayon drawings.

FOLK AND FAIRY TALES AND FABLES

These are tales of magic and enchantment, of kindly dwarfs and wicked witches, hard-pressed lassies and talking beasts, and there is one tall-tale hound dog that is pure Americana. Each generation clamors to hear these old tales and, in the modern illustrated editions, to pour over the colorful pictures which are as memorable as the stories.

SINGLE TALES IN PICTURE-BOOK FORM

Hans Christian Andersen: 55-59

55. THE NIGHTINGALE   Harper & Row
    Illustrated by Nancy Burkert

56. THE STEADFAST TIN SOLDIER   Scribner's
    Illustrated by Marcia Brown

57. THE SWINEHERD   Harcourt Brace Jovanovich
    Illustrated by Erik Blegvad

58. THE UGLY DUCKLING   Macmillan
    Illustrated by Johannes Larsen

59. THE WILD SWANS   Scribner's
    Illustrated by Marcia Brown

60. THE FAST SOONER HOUND   Houghton Mifflin
    Arna Bontemps
    Illustrated by Virginia Lee Burton

61. CHANTICLEER AND THE FOX   Crowell
    Geoffrey Chaucer
    Retold and illustrated by Barbara Cooney
    Caldecott Medal, 1959

                        Fables: 62-63
62. THE NORTH WIND AND THE SUN   Watts
    Retold and illustrated by Brian Wildsmith

63. ONCE A MOUSE   Scribner's
    Illustrated by Marcia Brown
    Caldecott Medal, 1962

                Jakob and Wilhelm Grimm: 64-69
64. HANSEL AND GRETEL   Knopf
    Illustrated by Warren Chappell
    Music by Engelbert Humperdinck

65. THE SHOEMAKER AND THE ELVES   Scribner's
    Illustrated by Adrienne Adams

66. THE SLEEPING BEAUTY   Harcourt Brace Jovanovich
    Illustrated by Felix Hoffmann

67. SNOW WHITE AND ROSE RED   Scribner's
    Illustrated by Adrienne Adams

68. SNOW WHITE AND THE SEVEN DWARFS   Coward-McCann
Illustrated by Wanda Gág

69. THE TRAVELING MUSICIANS   Harcourt Brace Jovanovich
Illustrated by Hans Fischer

70. THE WAVE   Houghton Mifflin
Margaret Hodges, adapter
Illustrated by Blair Lent

Joseph Jacobs: 71-72
71. DICK WHITTINGTON AND HIS CAT   Scribner's
Adapted and illustrated by Marcia Brown

72. TOM TIT TOT   Scribner's
Illustrated by Evaline Ness

Charles Perrault: 73-74
73. CINDERELLA   Scribner's
Illustrated by Marcia Brown
Caldecott Medal, 1955.

74. PUSS IN BOOTS   Scribner's
Illustrated by Marcia Brown

75. THE FOOL OF THE WORLD AND   Farrar, Straus and Giroux
THE FLYING SHIP
Arthur Ransome, reteller
Illustrated by Uri Shulevitz
Caldecott Medal, 1969

COLLECTIONS OF FOLK TALES AND FABLES

Aesop: 76-77

76. AESOP'S FABLES   Grosset & Dunlap
    Illustrated by Fritz Kredel

77. FABLES OF AESOP   Macmillan
    Joseph Jacobs, editor
    Illustrated by David Levine

These short allegorical stories in which animals are given human
characteristics in order to point out a moral are part of the world's
lasting literature. The use of individual fables with children is to be
recommended, for they are childlike in their emphasis on the simpler
virtues and in the impersonal quality of their telling.

78. ARTHUR RACKHAM FAIRY BOOK   Lippincott
    Illustrated by Arthur Rackham

79. EAST OF THE SUN AND WEST OF THE MOON,   Macmillan
    AND OTHER TALES
    Peter Asbjørnsen and Jørgen Moe
    Illustrated by Tom Vroman

80. EAST OF THE SUN AND WEST OF THE MOON: Viking
    TWENTY-ONE NORWEGIAN FOLK TALES
    Edited and illustrated by Ingri and Edgar D'Aulaire

Jakob and Wilhelm Grimm: 81-82
FAIRY TALES

The brothers Grimm were thirteen years collecting these tales in rural
Germany. To them, children are indebted for the well-loved HANSEL
AND GRETEL, SNOW WHITE AND THE SEVEN DWARFS,
RUMPELSTILTSKIN, THE BRAVE LITTLE TAILOR, and many

others. There are numerous editions of these stories, and the following are to be recommended. Their appeal covers a wide age range, and they are popular, too, with nine-to eleven-year-olds. Suggested editions are:

81. GRIMM'S FAIRY TALES   Grosset & Dunlap
    Illustrated by Fritz Kredel

82. TALES FROM GRIMM   Coward-McCann
    Freely translated and illustrated by Wanda Gag

83. ENGLISH FOLK AND FAIRY TALES   Putnam's
    Joseph Jacobs
    Illustrated by J.D. Batten

The favorite tales of the English-speaking world are in this volume. Among them are WHITTINGTON AND HIS CAT, JACK AND THE BEANSTALK, and some forty other familiar titles. Joseph Jacobs has retained much of the vernacular of the country folk, which makes these stories excellent for telling and for reading aloud.

RHYMES AND POETRY

84. TIME FOR POETRY (3d General Edition)   Scott, Foresman
    May Hill Arbuthnot and Shelton L. Root, Jr.

A fine anthology, unusual in its selection of almost eight hundred poems to be read to boys and girls four to fourteen. Poems are on subjects which appeal to children, and there is a special group, "Wisdom and Beauty," "to help young spirits soar." Selections range from the old nursery rhymes to outstanding modern poets and are distinctive for their melody, movement, and imaginative quality. There is a helpful introduction for adults on the enjoyment of poetry with children.

85. THE LITTLE HILL   Harcourt Brace Jovanovich
    Harry Behn
    Illustrated by the author

The poems in this small book range from gay nonsense verse for the youngest to authentic lyric poetry for the oldest children. Beautiful in format and content, this is a fresh and important contribution to poetry for children.

86. UNDER THE TENT OF THE SKY   Macmillan
    John E. Brewton, compiler
    Illustrated by Robert Lawson

A companion volume to SUNG UNDER THE SILVER UMBRELLA and to Mr. Brewton's GAILY WE PARADE, this anthology of poetry about animals is a choice one. With wild and domestic animals, insects, fish, birds, and "wee beasties" of every variety, these poems, both serious and humorous in mood, delight young children. Robert Lawson's illustrations add vitality and beauty to the verses.

87. THE BIRDS AND THE BEASTS WERE THERE   World
    William Cole, compiler
    Illustrated by Helen Siegl

The best introduction to this delightful collection of poems about all sorts of animals is the author's own at the beginning of the book. After relating the experiences of a man who tried to make a pet of a hyena, the reader may decide animal poems are safer. However, this is a serious collection with some nonsense verses about the beasts but also much about man's cruelty to animals which children need to encounter. Chiefly these poems sing of the beauty and grace of animals and the "honesty of their instincts," for this anthology is as sound biologically as it is poetically. It is a collection that belongs in every home and school library. OH, WHAT NONSENSE! (Viking) offers fifty "rib-tickling" poems illustrated with Tomi Ungerer's black-and-white sketches.

88. PRAYERS FROM THE ARK   Viking
    Carmen Bernos De Gasztold
    Illustrated by Jean Primrose
    Translated by Rumer Godden

Rumer Godden discovered the French edition of these twenty-seven verses and recognized their "exceptional genius and exquisite charm." Each is the prayer of a small animal to the Creator, expressing its special qualities of individuality and dependence, but always with acceptance and hopefulness. The poems, brief and poignantly lovely, have appeal for all ages.

89. COMPLETE NONSENSE BOOK   Dodd, Mead
    Edward Lear
    Illustrated by the author

"The Owl and the Pussy Cat," "The Pobble Who Had No Toes," "The Jumblies," and hundreds of other daft and delightful verses by Edward Lear have made nonsense verses popular both with children and adults since he began to write them in 1846. Lear's amusing illustrations make his NONSENSE BOOKS as much fun to look at as to read and listen to.

Alan A. Milne: 90-91

90. WHEN WE WERE VERY YOUNG   Dutton
    Illustrated by Ernest Shepard

91. NOW WE ARE SIX   Dutton
    Illustrated by Ernest Shepard

Perhaps the best light verse ever written for young children, these two books are full of nonsense, whimsy, and unexpected imaginings, but no fairies. The everyday world of the modern child comes gaily alive and is served up in dancing rhythms, with absurd words and jokes to add to the fun. Skillful line drawings by Ernest Shepard are a perfect accompaniment to the rhymes. A special edition with added color plates, THE WORLD OF CHRISTOPHER ROBIN, contains both the above titles in a single volume.

92. HAILSTONES AND HALIBUT BONES   Doubleday
Mary O'Neill
Illustrated by Leonard Weisgard

Distinctive rhythmic verses describe a dozen different colors and
explore in many dimensions the part each color plays in the world of
nature, play, and imagination. Leonard Weisgard has illustrated each of
the poems in tones of its own particular color in this stimulating and
highly original small volume.

93. UNDER THE TREE   Viking
Elizabeth Madox Roberts
Illustrated by F.D. Bedford

Written with deceiving simplicity, these poems of Elizabeth Madox
Roberts won her a poetry prize while she was still in college. "Mr.
Wells," "The Twins," "Mumps," "Water Noises," "The Worm,"
"Firefly Song" reflect a child's wonder about people and the world of
nature. Throughout these poems a child might be talking, simply and
gravely, about his experiences, but an artist has chosen the words and
ideas.

94. ALL THE SILVER PENNIES   Macmillan
Blanche Jennings Thompson, editor
Decorations by Ursula Arndt

Within a handsome single volume, newly illustrated, are SILVER
PENNIES, a favorite anthology of familiar poetry for over forty years,
and MORE SILVER PENNIES. Prefatory remarks give a feel for the
theme or spirit of each poem.

BIBLE STORIES
AND PRAYERS

95. SMALL RAIN   Viking
Bible Selections
Illustrated by Elizabeth Orton Jones

Verses from the Bible chosen by Jessie Orton Jones because of their
special significance for children. The illustrations by Elizabeth Orton
Jones interpret with simplicity and understanding the spiritual meaning
of the verses in terms of modern children's activities. A happy blending
of picture and text.

Bible Stories: 96-98

96. MOSES   Macmillan

97. DAVID   Macmillan

98. JOSEPH AND HIS BROTHERS   Macmillan
These stories of Bible heroes have special appeal for children because of
the dramatic movement of events. Maud and Miska Petersham have
illustrated the above attractive editions of the separate stories.

99. THE BOOK OF PSALMS, OLD TESTAMENT
Twenty-third Psalm

There is a reassuring, comforting quality about the Psalms which
children need. The Twenty-third Psalm, with its message of God's care
for his children, is usually the best introduction to this great body of
literature.

100. BLESS THIS DAY   Harcourt Brace Jovanovich
Elfrida Vipont
Illustrated by Harold Jones

This book of devotions may be used by the whole family. There are
little graces for the youngest, some of the matchless collects for
growing children and adults, and selections from ancient breviaries that
everyone should know. The prayers are grouped for waking, for others,

for guidance, for thanksgiving and praise, and for benediction, to mention a few. The illustrations by Harold Jones both in black and white and color are as full of grace as the prayers and add to the beauty of this choice book.

BIOGRAPHY

101. BENJAMIN FRANKLIN   Doubleday
Edgar and Ingri d'Aulaire
Illustrated by the authors

Full of homely details and wisely selected anecdotes, this picture-story biography serves as a convincing and appreciative introduction to a man who played an important role in our country's history. Maxims from the famous **POOR RICHARD'S ALMANAC** appear in marginal decorations on many pages. The author's **ABRAHAM LINCOLN** received the *Caldecott Medal, 1940.* Other favorites by these author-artists are **POCAHONTAS** and **COLUMBUS**.

102. THE COLUMBUS STORY   Scribner's
Alice Dalgliesh
Illustrated by Leo Politi

Leo Politi's numerous illustrations in glowing colors make this a handsome introductory picture biography for younger readers.

For Children 9, 10, and 11

FICTION

103. MR. POPPER'S PENGUINS
Little, Brown
Richard and Florence Atwater
Illustrated by Robert Lawson

Life in the Popper family was never quite the same after Mr. Popper received a penguin as a gift from an Antarctic explorer. This genuinely funny modern nonsense tale has readily won a place for itself among young readers. Excellent for reading aloud.

104. THE CHILDREN OF
GREEN KNOWE
Harcourt Brace Jovanovich
Lucy M. Boston
Illustrated by Peter Boston

When Tolly comes to Green Knowe to vacation with his great-grandmother, he finds the children who lived there in the seventeenth century. Sometimes he only hears them or sees them in a mirror, but sometimes he actually talks with them. So skillfully does the author move from one century to another that the past mingles with the present in the old castle where many generations have lived. Beautifully written and first published in England, this is a story for the imaginative child. Another distinguished story with the background of Green Knowe is a modern realistic animal story, A STRANGER AT GREEN KNOWE.

29

105. CADDIE WOODLAWN   Macmillan
Carol Brink
Illustrated by Kate Seredy

Life on the Wisconsin frontier in the 1860's becomes very real and vivid in this story of tomboy Caddie and her two brothers. Distinguished for its fine characterization and good background, CADDIE WOODLAWN retains a high place in children's voluntary choices of books. *Newbery Medal, 1936.*

106. THE FAMILY UNDER THE BRIDGE   Harper & Row
Natalie Savage Carlson
Illustrated by Garth Williams

Armand, a lovable old Paris hobo, lived a free, irresponsible life until three homeless children moved into his shelter under the bridge, and into his heart as well. He clings to his freedom as long as possible, but when the children ask Father Christmas to bring them a house, Armand becomes a workingman for the sake of his "starlings" and makes their wish come true. A heartwarming story told with lightness and humor, it brings the flavors and scenes of the Paris which Armand loved. The author's HAPPY ORPHELINE and A BROTHER FOR THE ORPHELINES are two other tales delightfully French in flavor.

Daniel Defoe: 107-9
107. ROBINSON CRUSOE   Scribner's
Illustrated by N.C. Wyeth

Being shipwrecked and cast ashore on a desert island is a fate most boys envy, and each generation admires the ingenuity and bravery of Robinson Crusoe in his struggle for existence. Although Defoe wrote this story in 1719 for adult readers, generations of children have claimed it for their own. Other recommended editions are:

108. LIFE AND STRANGE SURPRISING   Grosset & Dunlap
ADVENTURES OF ROBINSON CRUSOE
Illustrated by Lynd Ward

109. ROBINSON CRUSOE   Macmillan
Illustrated by Federico Castellon

110. THE WHEEL ON THE SCHOOL   Harper & Row
    Meindert De Jong
    Illustrated by Maurice Sendak

It was Lina, the only girl in the school, who wondered why there were no storks on the roofs of Shora, a small Dutch fishing village. Under the wise direction of the schoolmaster, plus the united efforts of the entire community, a wheel is found, and a pair of storks rescued from the storm-tossed sea set up housekeeping on the roof of the school. This author goes deeply into the heart of childhood and has written a moving story, filled with suspense and distinguished for the quality of its writing. *Newbery Medal, 1955.*

Charles Lutwidge Dodgson (pseud. Lewis Carroll): 111-12

111. ALICE'S ADVENTURES IN WONDERLAND   Macmillan
    THROUGH THE LOOKING GLASS
    Illustrated by John Tenniel

A highly imaginative master mathematician tells two stories of a little girl's dream journeys into lands of enchantment. Children share Alice's wonder as one magical event follows another, while grownups find keen enjoyment in the author's subtle philosophy and humor. The Mad Hatter, Tweedledum and Tweedledee, the Dormouse, the White Rabbit, the Red and White Queens, the Cheshire Cat, and other characters have all won permanent places in the child's book world. First published in 1865. Another recommended edition is:

112. ALICE'S ADVENTURES IN WONDERLAND   Watts
    Illustrated by John Tenniel

113. THE MATCHLOCK GUN   Dodd, Mead
    Walter Edmonds
    Illustrated by Paul Lantz

In his father's absence young Edward fires an heirloom gun and saves his family from an Indian attack. A well-known writer of historical fiction has based this dramatic story for younger readers on a true incident of the French and Indian wars. *Newbery Medal, 1942.*

114. THE MIDDLE MOFFAT   Harcourt Brace Jovanovich
Eleanor Estes
Illustrated by Louis Slobodkin

Janey was a serious little girl to whom surprising things always happened. Her mishaps performing in a play and at an organ recital are among the most sparkling chapters in this book. A humorous yet sensitively told story which shows true insight into the feelings of a medium-sized little girl and surrounds her with a real and convincing family atmosphere. Two other entertaining books in this series are THE MOFFATS and RUFUS M.

115. BLUE WILLOW   Viking
Doris Gates
Illustrated by Paul Lantz

Janey Larkin longed for the day when her family could once again enjoy real home life instead of their roving existence as cotton pickers in the San Joaquin Valley of California. A thought-provoking novel for younger readers, rich in social values and family and community life.

116. WIND IN THE WILLOWS   Dial
Kenneth Grahame
Illustrated by Arthur Rackham

Magic, beauty, and friendly humor are found in these unforgettable stories of small animal adventures first told by the author to his little son. Written with rare artistry, the book is a perfect reading-aloud choice for all ages. Distinguished illustrations by Arthur Rackham capture the spirit of the text. Another attractive edition (Scribner's) has pen-and-ink drawings by Ernest Shepard. First published in 1908.

117. KING OF THE WIND   Rand McNally
Marguerite Henry
Illustrated by Wesley Dennis

This is the moving story of the Godolphin Arabian that put his stamp on racehorse thoroughbreds, including our own Man o' War. In every one of her well-written animal stories, Mrs. Henry also creates unforgettable human characters. The little mute boy who guarded King of the Wind is a memorable example. *Newbery Medal, 1949.* Pictures by Wesley Dennis add appeal to this book and to the ever-popular JUSTIN MORGAN HAD A HORSE, MISTY OF CHINCOTEAGUE, and BRIGHTY OF THE GRAND CANYON.

Rudyard Kipling: 118-20

118. JUNGLE BOOK   Doubleday
   Illustrated by Kurt Wiese

Stories of the East Indian jungles and of Mowgli, who, although human, was adopted by the wolf pack and taught the laws of the jungle by Bagheera the panther and Baloo the bear. Other favorite tales in this volume are "Rikki-Tikki-Tavi" and "Toomai of the Elephants." First published in 1894. Other editions are:

119. THE JUNGLE BOOK   Grosset & Dunlap
   Illustrated by Fritz Eichenberg

120. THE JUNGLE BOOKS   Macmillan
   Illustrated by Robert Shore

121. RABBIT HILL   Viking
   Robert Lawson
   Illustrated by the author

Here is animal fantasy of a high order. Father Rabbit, a Southern gentleman of the old school, Mother Rabbit, the worrying kind, their son Georgie, and crusty old Uncle Analdas share in the excitement of the small creatures of Rabbit Hill when they learn that "New Folks" are coming to live in the Big House. "I do hope they're planting Folks," says Mother Rabbit, and so they prove to be, for they plant an extra large garden with plenty for all. The author has created a fresh, lively, and amusing world and has made drawings that are unusual in their careful execution and in their beauty, *Newbury Medal, 1945.* A sequel is TOUGH WINTER.

122. STRAWBERRY GIRL   Lippincott
   Lois Lenski
   Illustrated by the author

Young Birdie Boyer eagerly joins in to help her family work their small, newly acquired Florida backwoods farm. In addition, she starts a modest reform in Shoestring Slater and his shiftless, pesky family nearby! An authentic regional tale told with humor and vigor. *Newbery Medal, 1946.*

123. THE LION, THE WITCH AND THE WARDROBE   Macmillan
C.S. Lewis
Illustrated by Pauline Baynes

The distinguished author of THE SCREWTAPE LETTERS wrote this children's story for his godchild, and so began the NARNIA stories, outstanding modern fairy tales with an underlying theme of good overcoming evil. In this first title, four English children walk through the wardrobe in a strange home they are visiting and enter the cold, wintry land of Narnia, which is suffering under the spell of the White Witch. They are guided to the noble lion Aslan and loyally aid him in freeing Narnia and its inhabitants from their unhappy fate.

Carlo Lorenzini (pseud. C. Collodi): 124-26

124. ADVENTURES OF PINOCCHIO   Macmillan
Illustrated by Attilio Mussino

The story of a mischievous, saucy little marionette who finally became a real boy is just as beloved today as when it appeared in Italy over eighty years ago. Other suggested editions are:

125. ADVENTURES OF PINOCCHIO   Grosset & Dunlap
Illustrated by Fritz Kredel

126. PINOCCHIO, THE TALE OF A PUPPET   Lippincott
Illustrated by Anne Heyneman

127. HOMER PRICE   Viking
Robert McCloskey
Illustrated by the author

Where Route 56 meets 56A in the small midwestern town of Centerburg, Homer Price catches burglars with his pet skunk, copes with a ferocious doughnut machine in his uncle's lunchroom, and exposes the supercolossal comic strip hero, Super Duper. Text and pictures are pure Americana, hilarious and convincing in their portrayal of midwestern small-town life.

128. THE BORROWERS   Harcourt Brace Jovanovich
Mary Norton
Illustrated by Beth and Joe Krush

Fascinating fantasy about a tiny family that lived beneath the kitchen floor of an old English country house and "borrowed" from the larger human residents to fill their modest needs. Their sudden discovery by a small boy visitor almost proves to be their undoing. The imaginative details about the activities of the miniature people have tremendous appeal for children. Illustrations by Beth and Joe Krush are a perfect complement to this title and three others in the series: THE BORROWERS AFIELD, THE BORROWERS AFLOAT, and THE BORROWERS ALOFT.

129. OTTO OF THE SILVER HAND   Scribner's
Howard Pyle
Illustrated by the author

The story of Otto, the son of a German robber baron, and his adventures in a time of cruel war and deadly feuds. Howard Pyle has done some of his best work in this story of a gentle boy who held to his own ideas of right although they were opposed to the spirit of the age. First published in 1888.

130. HENRY REED, INC.   Viking
Keith Robertson
Illustrated by Robert McCloskey

In a genuinely funny modern tale, young Henry Reed, aided by twelve-year-old Midge Glass, launches into a free enterprise project to earn money during a summer holiday. With "research" activities ranging from earthworms to balloons, Henry and Midge achieve a highly profitable and well-publicized school holiday. Robert McCloskey's illustrations are as unforgettably and typically Americana as in his earlier HOMER PRICE.

131. VERONICA GANZ   Doubleday
Marilyn Sachs
Illustrated by Louis Glanzman

Overgrown Veronica, skilled in the use of fist and tongue, is the scourge of the eighth grade class. Not until undersized Peter comes on the scene, outwitting and enraging her by his shrewd anticipation of her every move, and then admitting his admiration for her, does Veronica begin to sense the importance of being a girl. A rewarding and humorous tale of an unhappy adolescent who discovers that it is more satisfying to be admired than to be feared.

132. BAMBI   Grosset & Dunlap
Felix Salten
Illustrated by Kurt Wiese

Bambi is a deer of the Danube forest whose story is told from the time he is a newly-born fawn until he becomes an antlered stag. The narrative is poetic, sympathetic, and filled with the forest sights and sounds which are part of Bambi's experience.

133. THE GOOD MASTER   Viking
Kate Seredy
Illustrated by the author

Motherless Kate was an irrepressible little hoyden until she was brought to her uncle's ranch and placed under his steadying influence and that of her cousin Jansci. The story of early twentieth-century Hungary is told with zest and humor by its Hungarian-born author-artist.

134. CALL IT COURAGE   Macmillan
Armstrong Sperry
Illustrated by the author

Mafatu overcomes his fear of the sea in a heroic gesture which wins back for him the respect of his fellow tribesmen of a South Sea island. The author's fine illustrations, dramatic narrative, and constructive theme make this a distinguished story. *Newbery Medal, 1941.*

Johanna Spyri: 135-37

135. HEIDI   Grosset & Dunlap
Illustrated by William Sharp

An old and well-loved story of the Swiss mountain girl Heidi, whose joyous nature wins the affection of her gruff old grandfather and all who know her. The simple story of her life in the mountain hut amidst the beauty of the snow-capped Alps has had a great appeal for boys and girls since it appeared in 1880. This translation by Helen B. Dole is considered the best. Other attractive editions are:

136. HEIDI Scribner's
Illustrated by Jessie Willcox Smith

137. HEIDI World
Illustrated by Leonard Weisgard

138. WINTER DANGER Harcourt Brace Jovanovich
William Steele
Illustrated by Paul Galdone

Caje and his father are completely at odds. The father knows only of the rough dangers of the hunter's life; Caje yearns for security and the ordered life of the settler-farmers. The boy gets his wish, but discovers that the only security in this world must be won the hard way by one's own efforts. This is only one example of William Steele's ability to make pioneer days vividly alive for modern children. In WILDERNESS JOURNEY, TOMAHAWKS AND TROUBLE, FAR FRONTIER, and other books, he shows stout-hearted boys blundering, learning, and growing in an adventurous struggle for survival.

139. HONK: THE MOOSE Dodd, Mead
Phil Stong
Illustrated by Kurt Wiese

When hungry Honk found shelter from the cold in a livery stable, not even the town policeman could budge him from his snug retreat. A cheerful winter's tale of an enterprising moose and the excitement he created in a peaceful Minnesota town.

140. MARY POPPINS Harcourt Brace Jovanovich
Pamela Travers
Illustrated by Mary Shepard

From the time that Mary Poppins, the new nursemaid, slid gracefully up the bannister, until, holding fast to her parrot-handled umbrella, she was carried away by the West Wind, the Banks children never knew a dull moment. This fantastic nonsense story and its sequels—MARY POPPINS COMES BACK, MARY POPPINS OPENS THE DOOR, and MARY POPPINS IN THE PARK—are favorite reading-aloud books equally enjoyed by girls and boys.

141. THE COTTAGE AT BANTRY BAY   Viking
Hilda Van Stockum
Illustrated by the author

The fairies are always just around the corner in Bantry Bay; and so it was natural that Father O'Sullivan's sprained ankle should start a chain of unusual incidents which ended with good news for everyone, especially five-year-old Francie, an always carefree, highly imaginative twin, who despite a crippled foot constantly led his gentler brother into mischief. A heart-warming story which presents a poignant picture of a close-knit village family in Ireland.

142. CHARLOTTE'S WEB   Harper & Row
E.B. White
Illustrated by Garth Williams

Here is that rare book, enthusiastically received and reviewed by both children and adults. The 'secret lies in the lucid style of that master stylist, E.B. White, and the unique story he tells of Wilbur the silly pig and Charlotte the spider, his faithful friend. When Wilbur hears about the fall butchering he has a pig-brand of hysterics until Charlotte promises to save him. Her methods bring utter confusion to the farm families responsible for Wilbur and intense satisfaction to the smug pig. Wilbur is saved, but Charlotte's death, if biologically sound, is indubitably sad. This combination of hilarity and compassion is good therapy and superb storytelling.

143. LITTLE HOUSE IN THE BIG WOODS   Harper & Row
Laura Ingalls Wilder
Illustrated by Garth Williams

An authentic story of a pioneer childhood in the Wisconsin woods and first of a series based upon memories of the author's own experiences. Together, these stories of Laura Ingalls, her family, and friends form a vivid chronicle of life in the early days of the Middle West. The series includes FARMER BOY, LITTLE HOUSE ON THE PRAIRIE, ON THE BANKS OF PLUM CREEK, BY THE SHORES OF SILVER LAKE, LONG WINTER, LITTLE TOWN ON THE PRAIRIE, THESE HAPPY GOLDEN YEARS.

MYTHOLOGY, FOLKLORE, AND FAIRY TALES

Hans Christian Andersen: 144-46

144. ANDERSEN'S FAIRY TALES   Grosset & Dunlap
   Illustrated by Arthur Szyk

Andersen was the most famous creator of fairy tales. He could discover a story in such inanimate objects as a tin soldier, a darning needle, or a broom; he could also write of such uncommon things as snow queens, mermaids, ice maidens, an ugly duckling, and a princess who could feel a pea through twenty mattresses and twenty feather beds. Other suggested editions are:

145. FAIRY TALES   Walck
   Illustrated by Tasha Tudor

146. IT'S PERFECTLY TRUE   Harcourt Brace Jovanovich
   Illustrated by Richard Bennett
   Translated by Paul Leyssac

147. STORIES OF THE GODS AND HEROES   Dial
   Sally Benson
   Illustrated by Steele Savage

Primitive man with childlike simplicity personified the mighty forces of nature and created stories about Apollo, the sun god, Athene, the goddess of wisdom, and Persephone, who was taken to Hades' realm. To the child, such myths are almost as entrancing as fairy tales, and the gods and goddesses become cherished acquaintances to greet with pleasure when they appear in later reading. Another good edition with unusual illustrations in the modern vein by Helen Sewell is BOOK OF MYTHS (Macmillan). Both editions are based on Thomas Bulfinch's AGE OF FABLE.

148. PECOS BILL   Whitman
James Cloyd Bowman
Illustrated by Laura Bannon

Cleverest and mightiest of all cowboys, Pecos Bill is the mythical hero of tales of achievement, related with sturdy humor around prairie camp fires in frontier days. Accepted as American folklore, this collection of tall tales has been appropriately illustrated in color and black and white by Laura Bannon.

149. THE KING'S DRUM AND   Harcourt Brace Jovanovich
     OTHER AFRICAN STORIES
Harold Courlander
Illustrated by Enrico Arno

A collection of African folk tales from the vast region south of the Sahara. Although animals are the primary characters, their antics invariably relate to some human condition of tribal society. The stories are marked by subtle humor, pathos, sly trickery, cruelty, honor, justice, and courage.

150. THUNDER OF THE GODS   Holt, Rinehart and Winston
Dorothy Hosford
Illustrated by C. and G. Louden

Boys and girls respond to the rugged quality of the Norse myths, tales of Odin, Baldur, Thor, and Loki. In this edition Dorothy Hosford retells them with strength and clarity, retaining their dramatic nature and infusing them with a rare understanding of the early civilization which first created them.

151. ARABIAN NIGHTS   McKay
Andrew Lang, editor
Illustrated by Vera Bock

Among the nineteen tales in this collection are the ever-popular "Aladdin," "Ali Baba and the Forty Thieves," and "Sinbad the Sailor." This particular edition is distinguished for its skillfully shortened versions.

152. YANKEE DOODLE'S COUSINS   Houghton Mifflin
       Anne Malcolmson
       Illustrated by Robert McCloskey

These folklore tales of Paul Bunyan, Pecos Bill, Ichabod Paddock, Johnny Appleseed, and others are part of the legendary lore of every young American. Their robust humor, absurdities, and exaggerations are a never-failing delight, and Robert McCloskey's drawings reflect these qualities to perfection.

153. MERRY ADVENTURES OF ROBIN HOOD   Scribner's
       Howard Pyle
       Illustrated by the author

Adapted from the old ballads, Robin Hood remains the children's favorite hero tale. Wrongfully deprived of his lands and title, Robin Hood, the Earl of Huntington, gathers about him a gay band of followers as stalwart as himself. In Sherwood Forest they wage war upon the cruel and greedy, right the wrongs of the poor, settle old scores in dashing style, and are eventually pardoned by the king. Their adventures, daring, humorous, and sometimes romantic, are enormously popular with children. Originally published in 1883. A distinguished edition using the original ballad form, SONG OF ROBIN HOOD (Houghton Mifflin), by Anne Malcolmson, has black-and-white illustrations, beautiful in design, by Virginia Lee Burton.

POETRY

154. BOOK OF AMERICANS   Holt, Rinehart and Winston
       Rosemary Carr and Stephen Vincent Benét
       Illustrated by Charles Child

From Christopher Columbus, the Pilgrims, and Miles Standish to the Wright brothers, Teddy Roosevelt, and Woodrow Wilson, these humorous poems highlight American history with uncanny skill. Some of the sketches are exceedingly funny, a few of them are serious and moving, and every one of them reveals the man with remarkable insight and completeness. This is a lively commentary on American history.

Walter De La Mare: 155-56

155. RHYMES AND VERSES: Holt, Rinehart and Winston
COLLECTED POEMS FOR CHILDREN
Illustrated by Elinore Blaisdell

156. PEACOCK PIE   Knopf
Illustrated by Barbara Cooney
Not since William Blake has anyone given us poetry for children of the quality of Walter De La Mare's. Admitting that even in his books for children there is much that is too enigmatic for them to understand, there still remains a rich residue of poetry they thoroughly enjoy. Full of fairy lore, a curious blend of reality and fantasy, ending often with a question unanswered or a mystery unsolved, these poems tease the imagination even while their melodies sing in the memory. Here is poetry that should be read aloud, heard and heard again, before it is fully savored. It is poetry to grow on.

157. FAVORITE POEMS OLD AND NEW   Doubleday
Helen Ferris, compiler
Illustrated by Leonard Weisgard
A rich and substantial anthology which captures varied moods and themes and includes many old favorites as well as recent poets. Illustrated with black-and-white stylized drawings.

158. FAR AND FEW: RHYMES OF THE   Little, Brown
NEVER WAS AND ALWAYS IS
David McCord
Illustrated by Henry B. Kane
David McCord is an experienced writer of verse for adults, and this

book for children shows his skill as a poet and his understanding of youngsters' moods and interests. The moods range from pure nonsense to quiet reflection. The lilt of the verses is varied and musical, from "A clickety fence/Give it a lick it's/A lickety fence" to the subtle rhythm of "Tiggady Rue" and the serene "The Star in the Pail." This book is one of the choicest additions to the children's poetry shelf in many years.

BIBLE STORIES

159. THE LORD IS MY SHEPHERD   Scribner's
Nancy Barnhart
Illustrated by the author

An edition of the Bible which will stir the imagination of boys and girls and lead the way to the Bible itself. The artist has selected favorite stories from the Old and New Testaments and, after years spent in Palestine and in research and study, has interpreted the stories in pictures of great strength and beauty.

BIOGRAPHY

160. BENJAMIN WEST AND HIS CAT GRIMALKIN   Bobbs-Merrill
Marguerite Henry
Illustrated by Wesley Dennis

A boy who found his colors in the earth, who made his brushes from his cat's tail, and who used poplar boards for paper, grew up to be called the "Father of American Painting." However, it took a meeting of the entire Quaker community to decide whether the young lad should be permitted to pursue the doubtful art of picture-making. This story of the boyhood of Benjamin West is written with an appreciation of the life, the customs, and the simple pleasures of the early Pennsylvania Quakers.

161. AMERICA'S ETHAN ALLEN Houghton Mifflin
Stewart Holbrook
Illustrated by Lynd Ward

A backwoods boy in a rough and tough region, during a rough and tough period, Ethan Allen proved his courage and the staunchness of his spirit. His was the driving force in founding the independent republic of Vermont, and, as leader of the Green Mountain Boys, it was he who planned the capture of Fort Ticonderoga. This is an exciting historical biography. The handsome pictures by Lynd Ward reflect the robust spirit of the period and illustrate the text with artistic power and deep feeling.

162. GOD'S TROUBADOUR Crowell
Sophie Jewett

A warm and sympathetic portrayal of the thirteenth-century apostle of brotherly love, St. Francis of Assisi, and the turbulent medieval period in which he lived as a merchant, soldier, and finally, humble Gray Brother. The illustrations are reproductions from the Giotto frescoes in Assisi.

163. THOMAS JEFFERSON: CHAMPION OF THE PEOPLE Follett
Clara Ingram Judson
Illustrated by Robert Frankenberg

In this biography little details of family living are interwoven, so the young reader sees Thomas Jefferson as a man to whom the goodness of home life and the confidence of friends were as important as his intellectual pursuits, his ideals of freedom for all, and his faith in a democratic government. As a lawyer, architect, musician, botanist, farmer, philosopher, and politician, he was the greatest creative genius of his time. This is one of several biographies of American statesmen by this author. In all of them Mrs. Judson achieves through thorough research a well-rounded and living portrait of a great leader.

164. RASCAL   Dutton
   Sterling North
   Illustrated by John Schoenherr
The author tells his own story of one unforgettable childhood year when he found a tiny raccoon in the woods and brought it home to become his inseparable companion. This distinctive autobiography offers delightful humor, a rare feeling for wildlife and the outdoors, and wonderfully warm characterizations of the motherless Sterling and his intellectual and preoccupied father. Its greatest appeal is for eleven-year-olds and through the early teens.

165. AMOS FORTUNE, FREE MAN   Dutton
   Elizabeth Yates
   Illustrated by Nora Unwin
Born a free man, the son of an African chief, Amos Fortune was sold into slavery and brought to this country in 1725. Becoming a tanner by trade, he bought his own freedom and, through hard work and sacrifice, that of others. At his death he was a respected citizen of Jaffrey, New Hampshire. This is the moving story not of a great statesman or leader but of a simple man, whose deep religious feeling and dedication to the fight for freedom make him an impressive individual. *Newbery Medal, 1951.*

For Children 12, 13, and 14

FICTION

Louisa M. Alcott: 166-68

166. LITTLE WOMEN   World
Illustrated by Hilda Van Stockum

Good stories of family life are always popular, but none has ever been more universally beloved than this classic written over a century ago. The four March girls and their mother are genuine people, delightfully individual. Children follow their struggles, fun, tragedy, and romance with as much interest today as they ever did. Jo is not only a favorite character but stands for the self-reliant, impulsive, enterprising young woman the modern girl admires. Other recommended editions are:

167. LITTLE WOMEN   Crowell
Illustrated by Barbara Cooney

168. LITTLE WOMEN   Little, Brown
Illustrated by Jessie Willcox Smith

169. THE BOOK OF THREE   Holt, Rinehart and Winston
Lloyd Alexander

"There are times when the seeking counts more than the finding." This philosophy of the author pervades this tale of Taran, Assistant Pig-Keeper in the mythical kingdom of Prydain, who, in his search for the oracular pig Hen Wen, becomes involved in a hazardous mission to save his country from the forces of evil. Inspired by Welsh legend and mythology, this well-written fantasy is the first title in the chronicle of Prydain. It is followed by THE BLACK CAULDRON, THE CASTLE

OF LLYR, TARAN WANDERER, and THE HIGH KING *(Newbery Medal, 1969)*.

170. THE INCREDIBLE JOURNEY   Little, Brown
    Sheila Burnford
    Illustrated by Carl Burger

The loyalty of animals to home and master is a familiar theme. But for sheer inventiveness, this story of a young Labrador retriever, an old bull-terrier, and a Siamese cat on a 250-mile trek through the Canadian wilderness is exceptional. These pampered house pets, each in his own way, share the hazards of the journey. Even the aloof and independent cat brings her kili to the old bullterrier after he is injured in a battle with a bear, and each resists the human beings who try to detain them from reaching their former home. The author's intimate knowledge of the ways of these animals gives credibility to a tale of intense drama and suspense, while the disciplined style makes a perfect read-aloud book.

171. THE WHITE MOUNTAINS   Macmillan
    John Christopher

This science fantasy is set a hundred years in the future. It is a powerfully told story of three boys who flee across Europe to the White Mountains, a natural barrier against the Tripods, merciless creatures who seek to control men's minds and make them docile slaves. This is the first book in an adventure-filled trilogy which tells of human efforts to discover the vulnerability of their strange enemies and to defeat them. The other titles are THE CITY OF GOLD AND LEAD and POOL OF FIRE.

172. THE WONDERFUL WINTER   Dutton
    Marchette Chute
    Illustrated by Grace Golden

Young Sir Robin Wakefield had a hard enough time with his three severe aunts; but when an unpleasant tutor was added to his trials, the boy and his dog set off for London. Half-starved, he finally blundered into Mr. Shakespeare's own theatre, where he was discovered by the poet, gently cared for, and taken into the home of actor John Heminges. Mrs. Heminges, the children, and even the boy apprentice all took kindly to Robin. He in turn blossomed in the warm, affectionate, and lively household. Eventually Robin was pressed into bit parts in the theatre, to his great delight, for he loved both Shakespeare and the plays. But by the end of his wonderful winter, Robin knew he must return to home and responsibilities. There is a triumphant homecoming and promise of a bright future for this winning young hero. A delightful picture of many aspects of Elizabethan London and the theater of Will Shakespeare.

Samuel L. Clemens (pseud. Mark Twain): 173-74
173. ADVENTURES OF TOM SAWYER
Macmillan
Illustrated by John Falter

In TOM SAWYER juvenile realism crossed the tracks for the first time to give children a casual glimpse of the seamy side of life. Tom's adventures involve Aunt Polly and her church-going friends on the one hand, Huck and his disreputable father on the other, and a hair-raising tragedy in the cave. Besides the absurd and hilarious episodes in this story, the mystery in which the boys become involved keeps this book a favorite with each succeeding generation. First published in 1876. Another attractive edition is:

174. ADVENTURES OF TOM SAWYER
World
Illustrated by Louis Slobodkin

Charles Dickens: 175-76
175. CHRISTMAS CAROL
Lippincott
Illustrated by Arthur Rackham

Ebenezer Scrooge, Tiny Tim, Bob Cratchit, and all the other characters of this well-known tale are as beloved today as they were over a century ago when this story first appeared. Another attractive edition is:

176. CHRISTMAS CAROL
Macmillan
Illustrated by John Groth

177. THE TWENTY-ONE BALLOONS   Viking
William Pene Du Bois
Illustrated by the author

Weary of teaching mathematics to the young, Professor Sherman equips a balloon and flies off in search of adventure. His journey ends suddenly when a hungry gull punctures the balloon and forces him down on the volcanic island of Krakatoa, rich in diamonds, unusual inhabitants, and explosive potentialities. A rare and imaginative pseudo-scientific tale told with great good humor and profusely illustrated by the author-artist. *Newbery Medal, 1948.*

178. JOHNNY TREMAIN   Houghton Mifflin
Esther Forbes
Illustrated by Lynd Ward

Revolutionary days in Boston found Johnny, a boy of thirteen, apprenticed to a silversmith. Accidentally maimed for life and unable to follow his trade, Johnny was caught up in the struggle for liberty. The author has a remarkable talent for transporting the reader to the scene; the wharves and streets of Boston, the Tea Party and what led up to it, and the fighting at Lexington and Concord are before the eyes as though the intervening years had been rolled aside. *Newbery Medal, 1944.*

179. MY SIDE OF THE MOUNTAIN   Dutton
Jean George
Illustrated by the author

An incredible story of a modern boy's life alone in the Catskill Mountains for one year. Making his home in the hollowed trunk of a hemlock tree, Sam Gribley learns to build a fire without matches, make a deerskin suit, and cook everything from frog soup to venison steak. This competent young "Thoreau's" descriptions of unforgettable experiences in the heart of nature make the book a delightful flight from civilization.

180. VULPES, THE RED FOX   Dutton
   John and Jean George
   Illustrated by the authors

This tale of the hunted and the hunters is an exciting contest of wits. Although the reader's sympathies are with the fox, he is prepared for the inevitably sad ending. Vulpes is the best of his kind, so intelligent and resourceful, so full of the zest of life that he actually courts the chase. He is shown from his cub days to his magnificent maturity. Beautiful illustrations enhance the dramatic quality of this enthralling tale, and the pictures and text will lead young readers to the authors' equally fine MASKED PROWLER.

181. THE LITTLE FISHES   Houghton Mifflin
   Erik Christian Haugaard
   Illustrated by Milton Johnson

Homeless Guido tells his own story of his efforts to lead two younger orphans from war-torn Naples to hoped-for safety farther north. Throughout the long journey the children encounter many people, both kind and cruel. This moving narrative of World War II is unforgettable for its depiction of a large cast of characters memorably described, and Guido, who is only twelve, stands out as a child of wartime whose many hardships develop in him a deep sense of compassion for others.

182. JAZZ COUNTRY   Harper & Row
   Nat Hentoff

Because Tom Curtis played the trumpet and was a jazz enthusiast, he became acquainted with some of the best black musicians in New York City. From them he learned the essence of jazz—the freedom, the emotion, the identification, the style. From them, too, he learned, as much as a white person can, what it means to be black, to sense the pent-up anger and frustration which they suffer. In the end, Tom goes off to Amherst College, still undecided whether to return to music or prepare himself to fight against the wrongs suffered by his black friends. An absorbing, thought-provoking story.

183. ACROSS FIVE APRILS   Follett
   Irene Hunt

Jethro Creighton is helping his mother plant potatoes on their southern Illinois farm when news comes that Fort Sumter has been fired upon. The Civil War stretches across five Aprils, from the year Jethro is nine until he is fourteen. He sees three brothers leave, one, after much soul-searching, to fight on the Confederate side. After his father's heart attack, all the farm work rests on Jethro's slender shoulders, but at the war's end, with the help of the local schoolmaster, he pursues the education he so ardently longs for. The warm family life and the characterization of each member give distinction to this book. Having heard stories of the war from her grandfather and having access to family letters and records, the author imparts an unusual sense of reality to the struggle of the Creightons during the long conflict.

184. SMOKY, THE COWHORSE   Scribner's
   Will James
   Illustrated by the author

Because Will James was a cowboy and knew a horse as only a cowboy could, this is one of the great stories of its kind, as well as a true picture of ranch life in the West. *Newbery Medal, 1927.*

185. RIFLES FOR WATIE   Crowell
   Harold Keith

To sixteen-year-old Jeff Bussey the Civil War promised to be a grand soldierly adventure. But the grueling years of small hardships and grave dangers, together with a strange set of circumstances which had Jeff serving in the Southern as well as the Northern armies, give the boy a new sympathy with all victims of war. A stirring and enlightening historical tale which does full justice to the Northern and Southern points of view. *Newbery Medal, 1958.*

186. BIG RED   Holiday
   Jim Kjelgaard
   Illustrated by Bob Kuhn

Between Danny and his father there was the warmth of sympathetic understanding, but between Danny and the Irish setter which was given him for training there was devotion that needed no words for expression. This is a distinguished story of the simultaneous development of a champion and a skilled trainer of champions and of the way they met Big Majesty, the bear which had long reigned supreme in the Wintapi wilderness.

187. ... AND NOW MIGUEL   Crowell
   Joseph Krumgold
   Illustrated by Jean Charlot

A regional story of deeply-rooted family life in New Mexico, where everyone from grandfather to uncles is a sheepraiser on land owned for generations by this family of Spanish descent. But this is also Miguel's story. For at twelve a boy is thinking of being a man, and to Miguel this would happen when he went with the men who take the sheep to the Sangre de Cristo Mountains for summer pasture. In telling how Miguel got his wish, the author shows a penetrating and perceptive understanding of a twelve-year-old boy. *Newbery Medal, 1954.*

Madeleine L'Engle: 188-89

188. MEET THE AUSTINS   Vanguard

Modern family life in a lively and sometimes turbulent household of four children from five to fifteen, as seen by Vicky, age twelve. There is laughter, tragedy, and adjustment to living with a spoiled, suddenly orphaned girl of ten, who is befriended by the Austins. Told with zest and understanding not only of growing children but of what makes a warm and loving family.

189. A WRINKLE IN TIME   Farrar, Straus and Giroux

The discerning reader who likes to be transported from the world of reality to the strange and mysterious will find this fantasy of space and time both original and fascinating. A brother and sister, together with a friend, go in search of their scientist father who was lost while engaged in secret work for the government on the tesseract problem. A tesseract is a wrinkle in time. The father is a prisoner on a forbidding planet, and after awesome and terrifying experiences, he is rescued, and the little group returns safely to Earth and home. *Newbery Medal, 1963.*

190. IT'S LIKE THIS, CAT   Harper & Row
   Emily Neville
   Illustrated by Emil Weiss

Dave Mitchell himself might have written this story, so real and natural is the portrayal of the inner feelings and attitudes of the fourteen-year-old New York City boy toward his parents, his friends, and a stray tomcat given to him by Crazy Old Kate, the neighborhood character. It is Cat who introduces him to two new friends, one a troubled college boy whom Dave's father guides to a greater maturity and the other his first girl friend. Any boy, even a reluctant reader, will take to this book eagerly, for it is written in a light, humorous style, the conversation is modern teen-age, and Dave's experiences are typical of many a city boy today. *Newbery Medal, 1964.*

191. ISLAND OF THE BLUE DOLPHINS   Houghton Mifflin
   Scott O'Dell

Because her brother had missed the ship that was taking their tribe to the mainland, Karana, a young Indian girl, remains with him. After her brother's death she lives alone for eighteen years on this wildly beautiful, treeless island off the coast of California. The struggle for survival is told in grim, realistic detail, alleviated by Karana's ability to find some comfort, beauty, and a measure of happiness in her solitary life. Based on the few facts known about an actual experience, the story is told with stark simplicity beautifully fitted to such a deeply moving experience. *Newbery Medal, 1961.*

192. THE YEARLING   Scribner's
   Marjorie Kinnan Rawlings
   Illustrated by N.C. Wyeth

This sensitive story of a lonely little boy, Jody, in the poverty-stricken wastelands of Florida is enlivened by an epic bear hunt, the boy's delight in his pet fawn, and his pride in the triumphs of his pint-sized father over their brawny neighbors. The final tragedy turns upon Jody's inability to face the cruel reality that his deer is destroying the family's scanty food supply and must be killed. The father's understanding and love make this story of growing up a little masterpiece.

193. CRYSTAL MOUNTAIN   Houghton Mifflin
Belle Dorman Rugh
Illustrated by Ernest Shepard

Four American boys living in Lebanon learn the language and grow to love the people of the country. The wild, beautiful mountains are their playground, and presently they discover an oddly built, empty house which fascinates them. A tomboy English girl proves a worthy companion and helps them rescue a mistreated pup, reform a brat of an American boy, and eventually solve the mystery of the deserted house. Excellent dialogue, vivid characterization of each child, and a lively story with unusual social significance make this a notable book.

194. THE WITCH OF BLACKBIRD POND   Houghton Mifflin
Elizabeth Speare

Headstrong and undisciplined, Barbados-bred Kit Tyler is an embarrassment to her Puritan relatives, and her sincere attempts to aid a reputed witch soon bring her to trial as a suspect. This distinguished story with its seventeenth-century background offers an absorbing historial romance of the tragic witch-hunting days in early Connecticut. *Newbery Medal, 1959.*

Robert Louis Stevenson: 195-97

195. TREASURE ISLAND   Scribner's
Illustrated by N.C. Wyeth

A dying pirate in a lonely inn starts young Jim Hawkins on a remarkable quest for buried treasure. This classic tale of the sea and hidden gold has no equal in adventure stories for young people. Originally published in 1882. Other attractive editions are:

196. TREASURE ISLAND   World
Illustrated by C.B. Falls

197. TREASURE ISLAND   Macmillan
    Illustrated by John Falter

198. DAWN WIND   Walck
    Rosemary Sutcliff
    Illustrated by Charles Keeping
Turbulent England during the invasion of the barbaric Saxon hordes is
recreated with superb historical imagination. After the last savage
battle, a fourteen-year-old boy becomes a thrall with a slave collar
about his neck. Given his freedom after twelve years of serfdom, he
goes in search of the half-starved waif of a girl he had earlier befriended.
But most important of all, he feels the first breath of the dawn wind
which promises the end of strife and a peaceful Christian homeland
once again. The narrative is handled with unusual skill by an English
author who has won the Carnegie Medal, which is similar to our
Newbery Medal.

199. THE HOBBIT   Houghton Mifflin
    J.R.R. Tolkien
    Illustrated by the author
It was some years before the children of the United States took to THE
HOBBIT. Now they are devotees like their older brothers and sisters. In
this book, as well as in the trilogy of THE RING, the fairy tale turns
into an allegory of Good and Evil, but this disturbs neither the reader
nor the hilarious action of the tale. The first chapter is a masterpiece of
confusion. The wizard Gandalf and innumerable dwarfs, descending
upon respectable well-to-do Bilbo Baggins, demand food, drink and his
aid on a perilous adventure. Bilbo has no intention of going, but he
does and becomes a hero in spite of himself. Humor, action, unique
characters, and compelling style make THE HOBBIT a must for good
readers—children and adults.

200. BANNER IN THE SKY   Lippincott
    James Ramsey Ullman
Not only does this story provide young readers with thrilling action,

but it gives them a memorable picture of the stern discipline, physical and moral, that goes into the making of a Swiss mountain guide. Young Rudi, though forced to work in a hotel kitchen, is determined to become a famous guide like his father. Secretly he cherishes the ambition to scale the Citadel, where his father lost his life, and to plant his father's red shirt on the pinnacle. Rudi's ups and downs are chiefly downs until he submits to rigorous training.

201. THE LONER   McKay
    Ester Wier
    Illustrated by Christine Price

A young migratory worker, without home or identity, is taken in by a lonely old woman, the "boss" of a Montana sheep ranch. He earns his name, David, after killing a grizzly bear, his Goliath, and after some time he becomes convinced that the ranch is his home. One dramatic episode, the death of a girl caught in a farm machine, is not glossed over, but neither is it morbidly emphasized. This is a fine, realistic story, sensitively told, and one in which both people and animals are strongly portrayed. For any adolescent who feels he is a "loner" this story will have special significance.

202. THESE HAPPY GOLDEN YEARS   Harper & Row
    Laura Ingalls Wilder
    Illustrated by Garth Williams

The author has written many of the experiences of her own childhood in this outstanding pioneer series, which begins with LITTLE HOUSE IN THE BIG WOODS for younger readers and concludes with this story of the heroine's marriage after a year of teaching. These books are a valuable contribution to the historial fiction of America's growth. Titles for the complete series are given in 143.

MYTHS AND LEGENDARY HERO TALES

203. CHILDREN OF ODIN   Macmillan
Padraic Colum
Illustrated by Willy Pogany

The Norse myths of Thor and Odin, of Loki the mischievous one, and of Iduna and her golden apples are retold in simple, rhythmic prose. Boys and girls like the strength and vigor of these old tales, and, because Padraic Colum has done his work directly from the Eddas, he has retained these qualities.

204. MYTHOLOGY   Little, Brown
Edith Hamilton
Illustrated by Steele Savage

A distinguished classical scholar presents a lucid, readable introduction to the theogony, myths, and epic tales of ancient Greece and Rome, including also a brief section on Norse mythology.

205. THE ODYSSEY OF HOMER   Walck
Homer
Retold by Barbara Leonie Picard

The noblest books intended for children tell of heroism, and children are by nature hero-worshippers. They respond to great words that clothe great thoughts and great deeds. Odysseus is admired by boys for his courage and resourcefulness, his sagacity, and his love of danger. The girls rejoice in the part of Penelope, the faithful wife, and in the emphasis on home and friendship. For younger children, THE ILIAD AND THE ODYSSEY OF HOMER (Macmillan), retold by Alfred J. Church, is a good introduction.

206. BOY'S KING ARTHUR   Scribner's
Sir Thomas Malory
Edited by Sidney Lanier
Illustrated by N.C. Wyeth

The fine ideals of chivalry and of disinterested service to a great cause are represented by the Knights of the Round Table. While their adventurous exploits provide the thrill of difficulties overcome and battles won, youth finds inspiration to be courageous, loyal, and faithful to a trust. This edition follows Malory's MORTE D'ARTHUR more closely than any other. Other recommended editions are BOOK OF KING ARTHUR AND HIS NOBLE NIGHTS (Lippincott) by Mary McLeod and the four volumes by Howard Pyle, retold in a more colorful, romantic style: STORY OF KING ARTHUR AND HIS KNIGHTS, STORY OF SIR LAUNCELOT AND HIS COMPANIONS, STORY OF THE CHAMPIONS OF THE ROUND TABLE, and STORY OF THE GRAIL AND THE PASSING OF ARTHUR.

207. PAUL BUNYAN   Harcourt Brace Jovanovich
     Esther Shephard
     Illustrated by Rockwell Kent

Tall tales of the mighty exploits of the legendary hero of American lumberjacks; of Teeny, his daughter; Babe, his great blue ox; and other woodsmen who range the forests from Maine to the Northwest. The robust vigor of the tales is graphically reproduced in the illustrations by Rockwell Kent. Another edition for the younger reader is OL' PAUL, THE MIGHTY LOGGER (Holiday) by Glen Rounds.

POETRY

208. AN INHERITANCE OF POETRY   Houghton Mifflin
     Gladys Adshead and Annis Duff, compilers

This choice collection of poems is designed for family use, which explains why many of the poems have special appeal for adolescents and adults. There are, nevertheless, exquisite selections for children, and the book makes a delightful addition to family reading.

209.THE GOLDEN JOURNEY: Reilly & Lee
   POEMS FOR YOUNG PEOPLE
   Louise Bogan and William Jay Smith, compilers
   Illustrated by Fritz Kredel

THE GOLDEN JOURNEY is probably the most distinguished
anthology for children and young people since Walter De La Mare
compiled his COME HITHER. Two gifted poets have brought together
favorite poems they themselves have enjoyed over the years—from
Shakespeare to e.e. cummings, and from William Blake to William Jay
Smith. These include a few poems for young children, more for
children in the middle years of childhood, and by far the most for the
oldest children growing into adolescence. It is a collection to grow to
and with, for here are poems to satisfy adults also. The format is
dignified and beautiful, and Fritz Kredel's woodcuts are just right.
Open this book to almost any page, and you will find a poem there that
will open the inner eyes of mind and spirit to life's absurdities or its
wonders—". . . thirty egrets wading—/Thirty egrets in a quiet evening."

210. POEMS OF EMILY DICKINSON   Crowell
    Emily Dickinson
    Selected by Helen Plotz
    Drawings by Robert Kipniss

Prefaced by a perceptive introduction to the life of Emily Dickinson,
here is a generous sampling of the nineteenth-century American
poetess's sensitive expression of nature, love, the inner life,
immortality, and the world around her.

211. REFLECTIONS ON A GIFT OF   Lothrop, Lee & Shepard
    WATERMELON PICKLE . . . AND OTHER MODERN VERSE
    Stephen Dunning, Edward Lueders, Hugh Smith, compilers
    Illustrated with photographs

Stimulating modern verse on an immense variety of subjects ranging
from nature to moods and to reflections and observations of the world
we live in. There is a brief provocative introduction on the reading of

poetry for enjoyment, followed by over a hundred poems of delightful diversity and distinctive quality.

212. YOU COME TOO   Holt, Rinehart and Winston
     Robert Frost
     Illustrated by Thomas Nason

More than any other poet, Robert Frost speaks for America with the voice and cadence of Americans. This is one reason why children should encounter his poetry early. The poet has made this a grateful task by choosing from his vast store this special selection of poems for children and youth. They may begin these poems at five, and they will still cherish them at eighty-five. For in spite of their seeming simplicity, they are rich in secondary meanings that do not occur to the reader at first. Meanwhile, this selection of Robert Frost's poems will give young readers a rare encounter with authentic poetry of high order.

213. LEAN OUT OF THE WINDOW: Atheneum
     AN ANTHOLOGY OF MODERN POETRY
     Sara Hannum and Gwendolyn E. Reed, compilers
     Illustrated by Ragna Tischler

The poems in this collection are not grouped under any subject matter classifications, but like the title poem they sing "a merry air" and represent a small but choice collection of modern poems. From such older moderns as Yeats and Sitwell to the more recent moderns such as Richard Wilbur, this inviting anthology should start young people reading more modern poetry.

214. THE SINGING AND THE GOLD: POEMS   Crowell
     TRANSLATED FROM WORLD LITERATURE
     Elinor Parker, compiler
     Illustrated by Clare Leighton

Poems from more than thirty different lands and a still greater range of centuries make this an invaluable collection of unusual poems. From the singing of men all over the world Elinor Parker has distilled the gold of their experience and their wisdom. The poems deal with the heroic, friendship, love, the seasons, solitude, sleep, and the other-worldly "all glorious above." For older children, youth, and adults here are poems not to be missed.

215. IMAGINATION'S OTHER PLACE   Crowell
Helen Plotz, compiler
Illustrated by Clare Leighton

This unique anthology for older children, youth, and adults is devoted to the poetry of science and mathematics, and all the sciences from astronomy to surgery are here. Each group opens with a relevant selection from the Bible. But this is not a solemn book. There are occasional limericks or nonsense verses, dramatic poems, and pure lyrics; and every poem has been chosen with a discriminating eye and ear for authentic poetry. Clare Leighton's illustrations and the beautiful format of the book add to the delight of the reader in exploring this treasure.

216. THIS WAY, DELIGHT   Pantheon
Sir Herbert Read, compiler
Illustrated by Juliet Kepes

"Poetry should be a deep delight," says Sir Herbert Read in a brief essay at the end of this distinguished anthology. Although poems written primarily for children are not found in these one hundred poems, which range from Shakespeare to Dylan Thomas, all the poems are within the young person's ability to understand and enjoy. The design, illustration, and format set a high standard of excellence in keeping with the content.

217. STARS TONIGHT   Macmillan
Sara Teasdale
Illustrated by Dorothy Lathrop

Lyric poetry about stars and night, coupled with Dorothy Lathrop's equally imaginative drawings, make this a choice book to read and to look at. Special favorites with the children are: "Stars," "Night," "February Twilight," "Falling Star," "Winter Moon," "The Coin," and "Redbirds."

BIOGRAPHY AND TRAVEL

218. JOURNEY TOWARD FREEDOM: Norton
THE STORY OF SOJOURNER TRUTH
Jacqueline Bernard

Born a Northern slave, then freed, Belle left her work as a domestic servant and set out on her travels, often on foot, to preach about her God and to attack slavery. In this new life she decided she would have a new name: Sojourner, "because I was to travel up and down the land," and Truth, "because I was to declare truth unto the people." Known for her wit and songs, she electrified audiences at religious and antislavery meetings, where she appeared with leading abolitionists. Powerful biography of a woman who became a legend in her time.

219. PATRICK HENRY: FIREBRAND   Little, Brown
OF THE REVOLUTION
Nardi Reeder Campion
Illustrated by Victor Mays

A lackadaisical youngster and an indifferent student, young Patrick Henry's domestic responsibility and growing concern for his country spurred him to heights of patriotism and achievement during the American Revolution. Well documented and written with disarming simplicity, as well as distinction, this book creates a stirring picture of an emerging nation and its leaders.

220. ANDREW JACKSON   Houghton Mifflin
Margaret Coit
Illustrated by Milton Johnson

The tough, peppery frontiersman who became seventh president of the United States of America comes alive in this vivid and enlightening biography, which shows why "Jacksonian Democracy" became a part of our heritage.

221. DANIEL BOONE   Viking
James Daugherty
Illustrated by the author

Upon the author's return from a trip through the Cumberlands, the

Smokies, and Boonesborough, he was inspired to tell Boone's story again because he believes that Boone and "his tough true breed are calling across a hundred years to young America." The spirit of the lusty, vigorous new country is in the rhythmic prose as well as in the illustrations. *Newbery Medal, 1940.*

Jeanette Eaton: 222-23

222. LEADER BY DESTINY   Harcourt Brace Jovanovich
   Illustrated by Jack Manley Rose
This definitive biography of Washington for young people makes use of recent research findings to create a vivid picture of a remarkable man. Revealing episodes in his early career show him sometimes humiliated and close to disgrace but struggling on to become the disciplined leader of men. The title of the book is also its theme—Washington called by destiny to play a role for which he had little taste. He forged himself into the leader he was called upon to be.

223. NARCISSA WHITMAN: Harcourt Brace Jovanovich
   PIONEER OF OREGON
   Illustrated by W. Ishmael
An unforgettable picture of a beautiful and courageous woman who, with her doctor husband, crossed the Rockies in 1836 to establish a mission among the Indians.

224. LEE OF VIRGINIA   Scribner's
   Douglas Southall Freeman
Douglas Southall Freeman won the Pulitzer Prize for his four-volume life of Robert E. Lee. This equally brilliant biography, written for younger readers, captures the warmth, spirituality, and courage of the great Southerner and creates, as well, an unforgettable picture of the Civil War days.

225. PENN   Viking
   Elizabeth Janet Gray
   Illustrated by George Whitney
In one of the finest biographies for young people, Penn is dramatic and

startling to most Americans. Gone is the sober, solemn Quaker, and in his place is the handsome, dashing son of Admiral Penn, head of the English navy. Young William Penn's conversion to Quakerism led to heartbreaking quarrels with the Admiral. William's courtroom defense of himself was an epoch-making event and a forerunner of the man's courageous and colorful maturity.

226. TOM PAINE: FREEDOM'S APOSTLE   Crowell
   Leo Gurko
   Illustrated by Fritz Kredel

A man for his times, Tom Paine fought with his pen for the rights of men during both the American and French revolutions. Humbly born and self-educated, he made history by his unique talents. Leo Gurko gives a distinguished portrayal of this controversial figure and the time in which he lived.

227. THE ENDLESS STEPPE: GROWING UP IN SIBERIA   Crowell
   Esther Hautzig

In June, 1941 ten-year-old Esther Rudomin's life amid a busy, loving, well-ordered Polish-Jewish household was drastically changed when the family, termed "capitalists and therefore enemies of the people," was herded into cattle cars and taken on a long, hard journey to Rubtsovsk, Siberia, where they became slave laborers for five years. This autobiographical account reveals the magnificent spirit that triumphed over the privations and degradations suffered. An outstanding story which has a great message for the heart and the mind.

228. KON-TIKI   Rand McNally
   Thor Heyerdahl
   Translated by F.H. Lyon

A spell-binding chronicle of the voyage from Peru to the Polynesian Islands taken by the author and five companions on a balsa-wood raft. The grandeur and beauty of the ever-changing sea and sky as well as the countless dangers which were their daily fare are recounted with seldom-matched skill. This memorable book, translated from the Norwegian, has many of the qualities of a classic.

229. CARRY ON, MR. BOWDITCH   Houghton Mifflin
     Jean Lee Latham
     Illustrated by John O'Hara Cosgrove II
A lively biography of a mathematician and astronomer who, before he
was thirty, wrote "The American Practical Navigator," still a standard
text in the U.S. Naval Academy. An undersized and undernourished
boy in a poverty-stricken home, Nathaniel Bowditch had to leave
school when he was ten. Apprenticed to a ship chandler in Salem,
Massachusetts, during the days of the sailing ships, he spent his nights
reading and studying by himself and later, when he went to sea, applied
his knowledge to navigation. An inspiring and animated account of a
man who with perseverance and singleness of purpose achieved success.
Newbery Medal, 1956.

230. ABE LINCOLN GROWS UP   Harcourt Brace Jovanovich
     Carl Sandburg
     Illustrated by James Daugherty
This biography includes the first twenty-seven chapters from the
author's ABRAHAM LINCOLN, THE PRAIRIE YEARS. It covers the
boyhood and youth of Lincoln, which Sandburg has recreated out of
his own feeling for and understanding of the prairie background from
which Lincoln came.

The Artist
and Children's Books

Much of the poetry of childhood depends upon the great talent and artistic insight that characterize illustrations for children's stories. The following eighteen pages contain black-and-white reproductions of some of the best present-day picture material for children's books. They are included in this bibliography through the kind permission of the artists and their publishers: Blackie & Son, Ltd.; Coward-McCann, Inc.; Thomas Y. Crowell Co.; Farrar, Straus and Giroux, Inc.; Harper & Row, Publishers,: Houghton Mifflin Co.; Charles Scribner's Sons; Vanguard Press, Inc.; The Viking Press, Inc.; Franklin Watts, Inc.; World's Work, Ltd.

MARCIA BROWN

Once a Mouse   Scribner's

Adapted by the illustrator   Illustration © 1961 by Marcia Brown

Marcia Brown is one of the most versatile of modern artists. She adapts her style to the mood and content of the story. The sturdy figure of *Dick Whittington* in earthy browns and black is precisely right for that hero. So are the flamboyant pinks for the dashing *Puss in Boots* and the delicately drawn figures in misty pastels for *The Steadfast Tin Soldier* and *Cinderella, Caldecott Medal, 1955.* But her book *Once a Mouse, Caldecott Medal, 1962,* differs from all the others. The artist has used the difficult medium of woodcuts with a posterlike effect that is boldly stylized and wonderfully interpretative of mood and action. The details in these striking pictures will reward a closer look. In rich jungle colors, the story of the rise and fall of an ungrateful mouse is as dramatically told by the pictures as by the text.

CONRAD BUFF
Dash and Dart
By Mary Buff

Viking

In their mountain studio, Mary and Conrad Buff study and make friends with the birds and animals of the forest. While Mary Buff writes, Conrad draws or paints. He is one of California's distinguished artists and his magnificent oils are to be found in some of the fine collections in galleries and private homes. His pictures range from the stark grandeur of Western buttes and mountains, so powerful that they are almost overwhelming, to the tender beauty of the forest in the spring or such a delicate detail as this sepia sketch of deer. This particular picture has the decorative quality of a Japanese print. You can almost see the thin-haired creatures flinching under the cold, wet snow.

VIRGINIA LEE BURTON

Mike Mulligan and His Steam Shovel   Houghton Mifflin
   By the illustrator

Virginia Lee Burton was a dancer before she was a successful author-artist. Perhaps this accounts for the swirling circular lines she uses to express action. Over and over again, the composition of her pictures follows this circular or elliptical pattern—from the forest and fights of *Robin Hood* to the evolution of a city in *The Little House*. In that book her crowding skyscrapers, elevated railroads, trolleys, and tracks do a whirling ballet in verticals and circles. Her personifications of runaway trains or plodding steam shovels follow this same pattern. And no one can personify boys' beloved machines more gaily and vividly than she.

BARBARA COONEY

Chanticleer and the Fox   Crowell

   Geoffrey Chaucer, adapted by the illustrator

For *Chanticleer* Barbara Cooney has used stylized illustrations well
suited to the precise form of the fable. In strong, bold colors she has
drawn the widow and her children, their little house, farm, and all the
animals. But on Chanticleer and his smiling enemy, the fox, she has
lavished glorious colors and decorative details that highlight these
handsome, well-matched antagonists. The medieval setting of "The
Nun's Priest's Tale," from which this fable is taken, is beautifully
realized in both the pictures and text. This is a book to reread, pore
over, and cherish. *Caldecott Medal, 1959.*

JAMES DAUGHERTY
Daniel Boone
By the illustrator

Viking

James Daugherty loves the great figures and the epic sweep of American history. He writes and illustrates with a rhythmic vigor that is well suited to the lusty heroes he portrays. His pictures are crowded and sometimes confusing. Details are subordinated to a single dominant impression—stark strength or savage action or wild gaiety or surging energy. The power in James Daugherty's illustrations is compelling. They are not pretty pictures, but they are memorable. *Newbery Medal, 1940.*

WANDA GÁG

Tales From Grimm   Coward-McCann
   Adapted by the illustrator

Wanda Gág grew up in a family that was steeped in the folk art of the
Old World. Her father painted in his spare time, and every child in the
family began to draw as soon as he could hold a pencil and manage a
scrap of paper. The old fairy tales she heard influenced Wanda Gág's
own writing and illustrating. Both have a unique folk quality. Sturdy
peasant figures appear in her pictures, and homely details of everyday
living. Strong masses of blacks and whites are balanced with a rhythmic
flow of lines that give to her compositions both strength and grace.
Children delight in exploring her humorous details, and adults
appreciate the tender beauty of her work.

THEODOR SEUSS GEISEL
The 500 Hats of Bartholomew Cubbins   Vanguard
    By the illustrator

Theodor Seuss Geisel, known as "Dr. Seuss," can turn humorous fantasy into beauty both in his stories and his pictures. His pop-eyed heroes, his impossible hats, fish, or birds, his stilt-loving royalty, or his wizards and nizzards have about them a beauty of line, a sudden splash of color, or a grace of movement that is utterly captivating. This is true of his landscapes as well. Seeing Theodor Geisel in his hilltop studio in California, with the city below him or the mountains, half lost in the mist, above him, one finds it easy to understand how dreams might come alive for him. But nothing except his own creative genius can account for the unique quality of his nonsense, which, at its most hilarious peak, has also beauty.

EZRA JACK KEATS
The Snowy Day   Viking
By the illustrator   Illustration © 1962 by Ezra Jack Keats
Small Peter's glorious adventure playing in the winter's first deep snow
is told in crisp, rhythmic prose and uncluttered illustrations, which
combine collage and watercolor and contrast brilliant and muted tones
with rare distinction. *Caldecott Medal, 1963.*

Little Georgie lay back in the warm grass and sang his song—

New Folks co-ming, Oh my! New Folks co-ming, Oh my! New Folks co-ming, Oh my! Oh my! Oh my!

ROBERT LAWSON
Rabbit Hill   Viking
By the illustrator

Robert Lawson ranks as one of America's outstanding book illustrators for children and is an author of distinction as well. His finely detailed drawings make his every character, human or animal, a genuine personality. His humor, whether robust, as in the drawings for *Ferdinand, Ben and Me,* and *Mr. Popper's Penguins,* or delicately sensitive, as in the illustrations for *Rabbit Hill* and *They Were Strong and Good,* unfailingly interpret the spirit of the story. Mr. Lawson has illustrated some thirty books, and he is the only juvenile author-artist who has won both the *Newbery* and *Caldecott Medals.*

ROBERT McCLOSKEY
Make Way for Ducklings   Viking
    By the illustrator

Lentil, the first book by the author-illustrator Robert McCloskey, was
quickly recognized as a choice bit of Ohioana. *Make Way for Ducklings,
Caldecott Medal, 1941,* and the later picture stories, *Blueberries for Sal,
One Morning in Maine,* and *Time of Wonder (Caldecott Medal, 1958)*
are similarly a part of the New England scene. In his chronicles of
Homer Price as related and pictured in *Homer Price* and *Centerburg
Tales,* Mr. McCloskey has created a character as truly American as Tom
Sawyer. With absolute integrity he describes and draws what he sees
and invests it with the kind of humor and realism that children
understand and persons of any age enjoy.

EVALINE NESS
  Tom Tit Tot

Scribner's
Illustration © 1965 by Evaline Ness

This author-artist shows versatility and originality in her illustrations, from the flat, bold color used for Rebecca Caudill's *A Pocketful of Cricket* to the broadly humorous, peasantlike drawings for the English folk tales *Tom Tit Tot* and *Mr. Miacca.* Her own illustrated story *Sam, Bangs and Moonshine* was the winner of the *Caldecott Medal, 1967.*

MAURICE SENDAK
Little Bear   Harper & Row; In Great Britain: World's Work
By Else H. Minarik   Illustration © 1957 by Maurice Sendak

Maurice Sendak's pictures of children fall into two distinct styles. His first illustrations for Ruth Krauss' *A Hole Is to Dig,* and for many succeeding books, pictured the antic grace of everyday children, cavorting like frolicsome pups. But in his own first book, *Kenny's Window,* both story and illustrations reveal a sensitive perception of the lonely, imaginative, inner life of children. This is evidenced again in his beautiful, full-color pictures of the moon-mad dancing children in Janice Udry's *Moon Jumpers.* And again his illustrations for Else Minarik's well-loved *Little Bear* books reveal the inner warmth and love of family relations. *Nutshell Library,* with its four tiny books written and illustrated by Mr. Sendak, is another example of this young man's creative gifts. One of these small books is a rhymed *ABC,* one a counting rhyme in accumulative form, one pure nonsense, and one a cautionary tale. The pictures, purely humorous, together with the text, will provide the youngest children with many a chuckle.

KATE SEREDY

The Good Master   Viking

By the illustrator

Kate Seredy once said that as a youngster in Hungary, she was in the
saddle so much of the time that she felt almost six-legged. Perhaps this
helps to account for the fact that she has a special gift for depicting
action both in the horses she draws with such power and the human
figures. Swirling skirts, blowing draperies, the light tilt of young figures;
hoofs off the ground, dust flying, or the bold stance of a spirited horse
—these convey to the beholder something of the excitement of
headlong action.

URI SHULEVITZ

The Fool of the World and the Flying Ship:
A Russian Tale   Farrar, Straus and Giroux
    Arthur Ransome, reteller   Illustration © 1968 by Uri Shulevitz

Warsaw-born Uri Shulevitz has illustrated a great variety of books by other authors as well as his own. He makes a special contribution to the field of folklore because of his colorful, imaginative drawings often touched with humor, as typified in this winner of the *Caldecott Medal, 1969.*

LYND WARD
The Biggest Bear   Houghton Mifflin
  By the illustrator

Lynd Ward's illustrations are both strong and tender. Often they have a three-dimensional quality that is curiously effective. His use of color in such books as *Paul Revere* is beautiful, but no more so than his powerful black-and-whites. The homespun character of the people in *The Biggest Bear, Caldecott Medal, 1953,* the chubby appealing bear cub, and appalling size of the full-grown animal in contrast to small Johnny, and the lovely glimpses of the forest make this book one of Lynd Ward's masterpieces, both droll and beautiful.

BRIAN WILDSMITH

A Child's Garden of Verses
By Robert Louis Stevenson

Watts

Whether in his superb *ABC* book, his fable picture books, or collections of poetry ranging from Mother Goose and Robert Louis Stevenson to *The Oxford Book of Poetry for Children,* Brian Wildsmith, English artist, has created a rich world of color in his illustrations. He believes that "children are fascinated by color and form," and his books contribute to their enjoyment and appreciation of these qualities.

GARTH WILLIAMS
A Brother for the Orphelines

Harper & Row
In Great Britain: Blackie and Son

By Natalie Savage Carlson   Illustration © 1959 by Garth Williams

Garth Williams' pictures add distinction to any book he illustrates. He works both in color and in black and white, but whether he is illustrating a fantasy—*Charlotte's Web*—or historical fiction—the *Little House* books—or the inimitable French children in the *Orpheline* series, his touch is sure, and pictures and text are one. People or animals, character, mood, and situations are revealed with tenderness or humor: Wilbur, the "radiant pig" taking off from the top of the manure pile; or stubborn, gallant Josine with the foundling in the pousette, fleeing madly ahead of the National Bicycle racers, who bear down on her like an avalanche; or Josine and Mme. Flattot brooding tenderly over the baby. Garth Williams' pictures *are* the characters.

TARO YASHIMA
Crow Boy
By the illustrator

Viking

The theme of a timid little Japanese school boy at last finding a place among his classmates is universal, as are so many of this author's books about children: *Momo's Kittens, Umbrella,* and *The Youngest One.* His lively illustrations are of Japanese children whether their background is in their native land or the United States. *Crow Boy* is especially appealing, both for its story and for the manner in which it captures the atmosphere of a Japanese village and the surrounding countryside.

Title Index and Price List

*Numbers refer to individual entries, not to pages.

Author-Illustrator Index

*Numbers refer to individual entries, not to pages.